CROCHETED HATS & SCARVES

CROCHETED HATS & SCARVES

35 STYLISH AND COLOURFUL CROCHET PATTERNS

NICKI TRENCH

CICO BOOKS

LONDON NEW YORK

Published in 2020 by CICO Books
an imprint of Ryland Peters & Small Ltd
20–21 Jockey's Fields, London WC1R 4BW

www.rylandpeters.com

10 9 8 7 6 5 4 3 2 1

Text © Nicki Trench 2020
Design, illustration and photography
© CICO Books 2020

Patterns in this book have previously
appeared in one of the following titles by
Nicki Trench: *Crochet Basics, Crocheted
Animal Hats, Crocheted Scarves and
Cowls, Cute and Easy Crochet, Cute
and Easy Crochet with Flowers, Cute
and Easy Crocheted Baby Clothes* or
Geek Chic Crochet.

A CIP catalogue record for this book is
available from the British Library.

ISBN: 978-1-78249-832-2

Printed in China

Editor: Marie Clayton
Designer: Alison Fenton
Photographers: Caroline Arber,
Terry Benson, James Gardiner,
Emma Mitchell and Penny Wincer
Stylists: Alison Davidson, Sophie Martell,
Rob Merrett, Luis Peral-Aranda and
Jo Thornhill
Illustrator: Stephen Dew

In-house editor: Anna Galkina
Art director: Sally Powell
Production manager: Gordana Simakovic
Publishing manager: Penny Craig
Publisher: Cindy Richards

Contents

Introduction 6

CHAPTER 1
EASY HATS AND ACCESSORIES 8

Baby Beanie Hat with Flowers 10
Nugget the Mouse 12
Ear Flap Hat 15
Rose Headband 18
Ribbon Hat 20
Baby's Pompom Hat 22
Peaked Toddler Hat 24
Pompom Beanie Hats 27
Turban Headband 30
Ribbon Baby Hat 32

CHAPTER 2
SIMPLE SCARVES AND WRAPS 34

Chunky Patchwork Scarf 36
Textured Neckerchief 38
Tweedy Scarf 40
Chunky Scarf 42
Skinny Scarf 44
Tasselled Baby Poncho 46
Wave and Chevron Chunky Scarf 48

CHAPTER 3
COLOURFUL AND FUN HATS 50

Beanie Hat 52
Baby's Flower Bonnet 54
Neil the Tiger 58
Baby's Sailboat Hat 62

CHAPTER 4
CREATIVE SCARVES, COWLS AND CAPES 64

Chevron and Daisy Scarf 66
Lace Scarf 68
Floral Lace Scarf 71
Wave and Chevron Stitch Scarf 74
Swishy Scarf 76
Chunky Seashell Scarf 78
Red Petal Cape 80
Beaded Ivory Scarf 84
Blossom Shawl 86
Mohair Scarf 89
Mohair Cowl 92
Silk and Wool Scarf 94
Fuchsia Shawl 96
Summer Evening Shawl 98

Techniques 100
Suppliers 112
Index 112

Introduction

Making hats and scarves is a brilliant way to practise your crochet skills, and every project we have included here has a skill rating. The first two chapters are devoted to quick makes and simple stitches. There are sweet hats and scarves for babies, such as the flower-adorned baby beanie hat on page 10 and the incredibly cute tasselled baby poncho on page 46, and there are colourful and versatile makes for adults, too. The textured neckerchief on page 38 is the perfect project for using up balls of yarn that you might have remaining from other projects, and the turban headband on page 30 is ideal for trying in different colours as it's so quick to make up.

When you're confident with the basics, you can move on to the projects with higher skill levels in chapters three and four. The baby's sailboat hat on page 62 is perfect for practising motifs, and the delicate summer evening shawl is made from a silk yarn that will be a pleasure to work with in the summer if you don't want to be using wool.

In case you're not quite sure what an abbreviation means, or how to do a particular stitch, the techniques are explained at the back of the book with step-by-step illustrations. If you want to use a yarn you've already got for a project, tension is given where essential, and the weight, length per ball and material blend of the yarn are also given to help you find a match. Hats and scarves make great gifts, so we hope you are inspired to get crocheting; pick up your hook, some yarn and off you go.

CHAPTER 1
EASY HATS AND ACCESSORIES

Baby Beanie Hat with Flowers

The perfect gift for a christening or a first birthday, this beanie hat is easy to make and will keep a little one's head warm and cosy.

YARN AND MATERIALS

Debbie Bliss Baby Cashmerino
(55% wool/33% acrylic/12% cashmere,
approx. 125m/137yd per 50g/1¾oz ball)
4ply (sport) weight yarn
    1 ball each of shades:
      101 Ecru (off-white) (A)
      001 Primrose (yellow) (B)
      002 Apple (green) (C)
      057 Mist (purple) (D)
      010 Lilac (E)
      100 White (F)
      601 Baby Pink (light pink) (G)

3mm (US size D/3) crochet hook

Yarn sewing needle

SIZE

Small: To fit age (approx.) 3–12 months
Large: To fit age (approx.) 1–2 years

FINISHED MEASUREMENTS

Small: 35.5cm (14in) around, 11cm
(4¼in) from crown to edge
Large: 40.5cm (16in) around, 12.5cm
(5in) from crown to edge

TENSION

18 sts x 13 rows over a 10cm (4in)
square working half treble, using a 3mm
(US size D/3) hook and Debbie Bliss
Baby Cashmerino.

ABBREVIATIONS

approx.	approximately
ch	chain
cont	continue
dc	double crochet
dtr	double treble
htr	half treble
rep	repeat
RS	right side
sp	space
ss	slip stitch
st(s)	stitch(es)
WS	wrong side

HAT

Using A, make 4ch, join with a ss in
first ch to form a ring.
Round 1 (RS): 2ch (counts as first
htr), 7htr in ring, join with a ss in first
2-ch. *(8 sts)*
Cont in rounds with RS always facing.
Round 2: 2ch, 1htr at base of first
2-ch, 2htr in each st to end, join with
a ss in top of first 2-ch. *(16 sts)*
Round 3: 2ch, 1htr at base of first
2-ch, *1htr in next st, 2htr in next st;
rep from * to last st, 1htr in last st, join
with a ss in top of first 2-ch. *(24 sts)*
Round 4: Rep Round 3. *(36 sts)*
Round 5: 2ch, 1htr at base of first
2-ch, *1htr in each of next 2 sts, 2htr
in next st; rep from * to last 2 sts, 1htr
in each of last 2 sts, join with a ss in
top of first 2-ch. *(48 sts)*

SMALL SIZE ONLY:

Round 6: 2ch, 1htr at base of first
2-ch, *1htr in each of next 7 sts, 2htr
in next st; rep from * to last 7 sts, 1htr
in each st to end, join with a ss in top
of first 2-ch. *(54 sts)*
Round 7: 2ch, 1htr at base of first
2-ch, *1htr in each of next 8 sts, 2htr
in next st; rep from * to last 8 sts, 1htr
in each st to end, join with a ss in top
of first 2-ch. *(60 sts)*
Rounds 8–14: 2ch, 1htr in each st to
end, join with a ss in first 2-ch. *(60 sts)*
Fasten off A.
Round 15: Join B with a ss in any htr,
1ch, 1dc in each st to end, join with a
ss in first dc.
Round 16: 1ch, 1dc in each st to
end, join with a ss in first dc.
Fasten off.

LARGE SIZE ONLY:

Round 6: 2ch, 1htr at base of first
2-ch, *1htr in each of next 3 sts, 2htr
in next st; rep from * to last 3 sts, 1htr
in each st to end, join with a ss in top
of first 2-ch. *(60 sts)*
Round 7: 2ch, 1htr at base of first
2-ch, *1htr in each of next 5 sts, 2htr
in next st; rep from * to last 5 sts, 1htr
in each st to end, join with a ss in top
of first 2-ch. *(70 sts)*
Rounds 8–18: 2ch, 1htr in each st to
end, join with a ss in top of first 2-ch.
(70 sts)
Fasten off A.

Round 19: Join B with a ss in any htr,
1ch, 1dc in each st to end, join with a
ss in first dc.
Round 20: 1ch, 1dc in each st to
end, join with a ss in first dc.
Fasten off.

FLOWERS

(make 7 or 8 using any two of B, C, D,
E, F and G for each)
Using first colour, 4ch, join with a ss in
first ch to form a ring.
Round 1 (RS): 1ch, 5dc in ring, cut
off first colour, join second colour with
a ss in first dc.
Round 2: *[4ch, 1dtr, 4ch, 1ss] in next
st; rep from * 5 times more (6 petals),
working last ss in dc at base of first
4-ch.
Fasten off.
Sew in ends.

FINISHING

Block and starch flowers.

STALKS:

Using same colour yarn as Round 1 of
flower, join yarn with a ss in any two
loops at back of flower (WS) near
centre of Round 1.
Make between 4 and 6 ch for stalk (to
vary length of stalks), then with RS of
hat facing, join flower with a ss in any
two loops to centre of top of hat
(attaching flowers around outside of
Round 1).
Fasten off and sew in ends.
Attach all flowers in the same way.

Nugget the Mouse

Little round ears and a cute nose! The nose is stuffed with polyester filling, or use yarn ends from your stash.

SKILL RATING: ● ● ●

YARN AND MATERIALS

Debbie Bliss Cashmerino Aran (55% merino wool/33% acrylic/12% cashmere, approx. 90m/98yd per 50g/1¾oz ball) Aran (worsted) weight yarn
    1 ball of shade 009 Grey (MC)
    Small amount of shade 603 Baby Pink (pale pink) (A)

Debbie Bliss Baby Cashmerino (55% wool/33% acrylic/12% cashmere, approx. 125m/137yd per 50g/1¾oz ball) 4ply (sport) weight yarn
    Scrap of shade 078 Lipstick Pink (deep pink) (B)

Debbie Bliss Rialto DK (100% merino wool, approx. 105m/115yd per 50g/1¾oz ball) DK (light worsted) weight yarn
    Scraps of each of shades:
    001 White (C)
    003 Black (D)

5mm (US size H/8) and 3.5mm (US size E/4) crochet hooks

Yarn sewing needle

100% polyester toy stuffing

SIZE

To fit age 6–24 months

FINISHED MEASUREMENTS

Approx. 40.5–46cm (16–18in) around, 16.5cm (6½in) from crown to edge

TENSION

15 sts x 11 rows over a 10cm (4in) square working double crochet, using a 5mm (US size H/8) hook and Debbie Bliss Cashmerino Aran.

ABBREVIATIONS

approx.	approximately
beg	beginning
ch	chain
cont	continue
dc	double crochet
foll	following
htr	half treble
MC	main colour
rep	repeat
RS	right side
ss	slip stitch
st(s)	stitch(es)
tr	treble
WS	wrong side

HAT

Work in rounds, placing st marker at beg of each round.

Round 1: Using MC and 5mm (US size H/8) hook, 2ch, 8htr in second ch from hook. *(8 sts)*

Round 2: 2htr in each st. *(16 sts)*

Round 3: *1htr in next st, 2htr in next st; rep from * to end. *(24 sts)*

Round 4: *1htr in each of next 2 sts, 2htr in next st; rep from * to end. *(32 sts)*

Round 5: *1htr in each of next 3 sts, 2htr in next st; rep from * to end. *(40 sts)*

Round 6: *1htr in each of next 4 sts, 2htr in next st; rep from * to end. *(48 sts)*

Round 7: *1htr in each of next 5 sts, 2htr in next st; rep from * to end. *(56 sts)*

Round 8: *1htr in each of next 6 sts, 2htr in next st; rep from * to end. *(64 sts)*

Rounds 9–19: 1htr in each st to end. *(64 sts, or until work measures approx. 16.5cm/6½in) from start)*

Next round: 1dc in each st, ss in last st. Fasten off.

EARS

(make 4)

Work in rounds, placing st marker at beg of each round.

Using A and 5mm (US size H/8) hook, make 4ch, join with a ss to form a ring.

Round 1: 1ch, 12dc in ring, cut A, using MC, join with a ss in first dc. *(12 sts)*

Round 2: Cont with MC, 1ch, 2dc in same st as ss and each foll st to end, join with a ss in first dc. *(24 sts)*

Round 3: 1ch, 1dc in same st as ss, 1dc in each of next 2 sts, 2dc in next st, *1dc in each of next 3 sts, 2dc in next st; rep from * to end, join with a ss in first dc. *(30 sts)*

Round 4: 1ch, 1dc in first st, 1dc in each foll st to end. Join with a ss in first dc. *(30 sts)*

Fasten off, leaving a long tail for sewing on later.

NOSE

Work in rounds, placing st marker at beg of each round.

Round 1: Using MC and 3.5mm (US size E/4) hook, 2ch, 4dc in second ch from hook. *(4 sts)*

Round 2: 2dc in each st to end. *(8 sts)*

Round 3: *1dc in next st, 2dc in next st; rep from * to end. *(12 sts)*

Round 4: *1dc in each of next 2 sts, 2dc in next st; rep from * to end. *(16 sts)*

Round 5: *1dc in each of next 3 sts, 2dc in next st; rep from * to end. *(20 sts)*

Rounds 6–8: 1dc in each st to end.

Fasten off, leaving a long tail for sewing on.

NOSE TIP

Using B and 3.5mm (US size E/4) hook, make 2ch, 5tr in second ch from hook.

Fasten off, leaving a long end.

FINISHING

Sew around the hole in the centre of the ears and pull to close. Place two ears with WS together, then sew each pair of ears on at the centre top of the hat approx. 7.5cm (3in) apart and starting approx. 4 rounds down from the top.

Stuff the nose, position it in the centre of the hat at the bottom edge and sew in place.

Sew around the opening of the nose tip to close and make it into a bobble shape. Sew onto the tip of the nose.

Using C, sew 3 whiskers in straight stitch (see page 111) on each side of nose, using the photo as a guide.

Using D, embroider eyes in satin stitch (see page 111), using D, approx. 1 row above the nose and 7 sts apart.

Ear Flap Hat

Look stylish, while keeping your ears warm at the same time, with this fashionable hat.

SKILL RATING: ● ● ●

YARN AND MATERIALS

HAT:
Debbie Bliss Cashmerino Aran (55% merino wool/33% acrylic/ 12% cashmere, approx. 90m/98yd per 50g/1¾oz ball) Aran (worsted) weight yarn
    3 balls of shade 027 Oatmeal (pale blue) (A)
    1 ball of shade 048 Burnt Orange (orange) (B)

FLOWERS:
Debbie Bliss Rialto DK (100% merino wool, approx. 105m/115yd per 50g/1¾oz ball) DK (light worsted) weight yarn
    Small amounts each of shades 057 Banana (yellow) (C) and 002 Ecru (white) (D)

3mm (US size D/3), 5mm (US size H/8) and 6mm (US size J/10) crochet hooks

Yarn sewing needle

FINISHED MEASUREMENTS
Small: 50cm (20in) around
Large: 54.5cm (21¾in) around

TENSION
11 sts x 9 rows over a 10cm (4in) square working half treble, using a 6mm (US size J/10) hook and two strands of Debbie Bliss Cashmerino Aran.

ABBREVIATIONS

approx.	approximately
ch	chain
cont	continu(e)(ing)
dc	double crochet
dtr	double treble
htr	half treble
rep	repeat
RS	right side
ss	slip stitch
st(s)	stitch(es)
yrh	yarn round hook

SPECIAL ABBREVIATION

htr2tog (half treble 2 stitches together): [yrh, insert hook in next st, yrh, pull yarn through] twice (5 loops on hook), yrh, pull through all 5 loops on hook

Note: The hat is made starting from top down and worked in a spiral. Mark the beginning and end of each round by inserting a stitch marker in the loop on the hook at the beginning of each round.

TIP
Use the yarn double by using two balls of yarn, with one strand from each held together.

HAT

Using a double strand of A and 6mm (US size J/10) hook, make 3ch.
Round 1 (RS): 9htr in 3rd ch from hook (missed 2-ch counts as first htr).
(10 sts)
Cont in rounds with RS always facing.
Round 2: 2htr in top of 2-ch at beg of Round 1, 2htr in each of next 9 htr.
(20 sts)
Round 3: *1htr in next st, 2htr in next st; rep from * to end. *(30 sts)*
Round 4: *1htr in each of next 2 sts, 2htr in next st; rep from * to end. *(40 sts)*
Round 5: *1htr in each of next 3 sts, 2htr in next st; rep from * to end. *(50 sts)*

SMALL SIZE ONLY:

Round 6: *1htr in each of next 9 sts, 2htr in next st; rep from * to end. *(55 sts)*
Round 7: *1htr in each st to end.
Rounds 8–15: Rep Round 7.

LARGE SIZE ONLY:

Round 6: *1htr in each of next 4 sts, 2htr in next st; rep from * to end. *(60 sts)*
Round 7: *1htr in each st to end.
Rounds 8–17: Rep Round 7.

BOTH SIZES:

Fasten off one strand only, do not cut off second strand. Cont working with one strand of yarn only and using 5mm (US size H/8) hook.

FIRST EAR FLAP:

Put st marker in loop on hook.

*With RS facing, 1htr in each of next 12 sts, turn.

Next row: 2ch, htr2tog over first two sts, 1htr in each of next 8 sts, htr2tog. *(10 sts)*

Next row: 2ch, htr2tog, 1htr in each of next 6 sts, htr2tog. *(8 sts)*

Next row: 2ch, htr2tog, 1htr in each of next 4 sts, htr2tog. *(6 sts)*

Next row: 2ch, htr2tog, 1htr in each of next 2 sts, htr2tog. *(4 sts)*

Fasten off.

SECOND EAR FLAP:

With RS facing and using 5mm (US size H/8) hook and one strand of A only, fold hat flat and on opposite side to first flap, join yarn with a ss in st to correspond with last st of first row (of first flap), place st marker in loop, 1ch; rep from * of First Ear Flap.

EDGING:

Round 1 (RS): Using one strand of B and 5mm (US size H/8) hook, join yarn with a ss in first st of first flap, 1ch, 1dc in same place as ss, work a total of 20 dc evenly around flap (working 2dc in corners), 1dc in each st to next flap, work 20dc evenly around flap (working 2dc in corners), 1dc in each st to end, join with a ss in first dc.

Fasten off.

FLOWERS

(make 2)

Using C and 3mm (US size D/3) hook, make 4ch, join with a ss in first ch to form a ring.

Round 1 (RS): 1ch, 18dc in ring, cut off C, join D with a ss in first dc.

Cont with RS facing.

Round 2: [4ch, 1dtr in next st, 4ch, 1ss in next st] 9 times, working last ss at base of first 4-ch. *(9 petals)*

Fasten off.

FINISHING

Sew in the ends on the hat.

Close the hole in the centre of the flowers by sewing around the centre with the tail of yarn C. Sew in the ends to tidy up the flower.

Block, starch and press the flowers.

Arrange the flowers on one side at the front of the hat and sew in place.

Rose Headband

This flower headband is a quick and easy project so is ideal for beginners. It can be made in a couple of hours and is perfect to keep your ears warm when you don't want to wear a hat.

SKILL RATING: ● ● ●

YARN AND MATERIALS

Debbie Bliss Cashmerino Aran (55% merino wool/33% acrylic/12% cashmere, approx. 90m/98yd per 50g/1¾oz ball) Aran (worsted) weight yarn

1 ball each of shades:
027 Oatmeal (pale grey) (A)
610 Ruby (dark red) (B)

5mm (US size H/8) crochet hook

Yarn sewing needle

SIZE

One size, but length is adjustable to fit any head size

FINISHED MEASUREMENTS

49 x 9.5cm (19¼ x 3¾in)

TENSION

16 sts x 10 rows over a 10cm (4in) square working half treble, using a 5mm (US size H/8) hook and Debbie Bliss Cashmerino Aran.

ABBREVIATIONS

approx. approximately
ch chain
ch sp(s) chain space(s)
cont continue
dc double crochet
htr half treble
rep repeat
RS right side
ss slip stitch
st(s) stitch(es)
tr treble

HAT

Using A, make 15ch.
Row 1: 1dc in 2nd ch from hook, 1dc in each ch to end. *(14 sts)*
Row 2: 2ch, 1htr in each dc to end.
Row 3: 2ch, 1htr in each htr to end.
Row 4: 1ch, 1dc in each htr to end.
Row 5: 1ch, 1dc in each dc to end.
Rep Rows 2–5 until work measures approx. 49cm (19¼in), or to fit around head.
Fasten off.

GATHERING STRAP

Using A, make 11ch.
Row 1: 1htr in 3rd ch from hook, 1htr in each ch to end. *(9 htr)*
Row 2: 2ch, 1htr in each htr to end.
Rep Row 2 six times more.
Fasten off.

FLOWER

Using B, make 55ch.
Row 1 (RS): 1tr in 5th ch from hook, *1ch, miss 1 ch, [1tr, 1ch, 1tr] in next ch; rep from * to end of row.
Row 2: 3ch, 5tr in first 1-ch sp, *1dc in next 1-ch sp, 6tr in next ch sp; rep from *, working last 6tr in last ch sp. *(25 shells)*
Fasten off, leaving a long tail for sewing flower together.

FINISHING

Fold the headband in half with RS together, so the short ends meet. Using A, join the ends together with a double crochet seam, working 1dc in each st through both layers. Fasten off.

Turn the headband RS out and sew in the end.

Fold the headband gathering strap around the headband so it covers the seam and join the ends together with a double crochet seam as for the headband seam. Twist the strap around so its seam is inside the headband. Sew in any ends.

FLOWER:
To finish the flower, thread the needle with the yarn tail and weave down the side of the shell to the bottom. Roll the first shell tightly to form the centre bud. Stitch at the base of the shell with two stitches to hold it in place, then roll the remaining strip around the bud to form the rose, securing as you roll by stitching through the layers of chains at the bottom of the rose. Sew the rose in position onto the headband gathering strap. Sew in any ends.

TIP

Make the headband in a colour to match your outfit for an eye-catching effect.

Ribbon Hat

A fun, easy hat that can be dressed up with a length of pretty ribbon – or you could use plaited wool or a strip of lovely vintage fabric.

SKILL RATING: ● ● ●

YARN AND MATERIALS

Rooster Almerino DK (50% baby alpaca/50% merino wool, approx. 113m/124yd per 50g/1¾oz ball) DK (light worsted) weight yarn
    2 balls of shade 206 Caviar (grey)

4mm (US size G/6) crochet hook

Yarn sewing needle

1m (40in) of 12mm (½in) wide ribbon

SIZE

One size

FINISHED MEASUREMENTS

51cm (20in) around, 25.5cm (10in) from crown to edge

TENSION

15 sts x 12 rows over a 10cm (4in) square working half treble, using a 4mm (US size G/6) hook and Rooster Almerino DK.

ABBREVIATIONS

approx. approximately
ch chain
htr half treble
rep repeat
sp space
ss slip stitch
st(s) stitch(es)
tr treble
yrh yarn round hook

SPECIAL ABBREVIATIONS

rt/rf (raised treble round front): yrh, insert hook from front and around post (stem) of next tr from right to left, yrh, pull yarn through work, [yrh, pull yarn through first 2 loops on hook] twice

rt/rb (raised treble round back): yrh, insert hook from back and around post (stem) of next tr from right to left, yrh, pull yarn through work, [yrh, pull yarn through first 2 loops on hook] twice

HAT

Make 76ch, join with a ss in first ch to form a ring.
Round 1: 3ch (counts as 1tr here and throughout), 1tr in each ch, join with a ss in top of 3-ch. *(76 tr)*
Round 2: 3ch, miss first st, *rt/rf around next tr from Round 1, rt/rb around next tr from Round 1; rep from * to end, rt/rf around last tr from Round 1, join with a ss in top of 3-ch.
Round 3: Rep Round 2.
Round 4: 2ch, miss first st, 1htr in each st to end, join with a ss in top of 2-ch.
Rounds 5–25: Rep Round 4.
Round 26 (eyelet round): 3ch, miss next st, *1htr in each of next 3 sts, 1ch, miss next st; rep from * to last 2 sts, 1htr in each of last 2 sts, join with a ss in 2nd ch of 3-ch.
Round 27: 2ch, *1htr in ch-1 sp, 1htr in each of next 3 sts; rep from * to end omitting 1htr at end of last rep, join with a ss in top of 2-ch.
Rounds 28–31: 2ch, 1htr in each st to end, join with a ss in top of 2-ch.
Fasten off.

FINISHING

Sew in all ends.

Weave a ribbon through the eyelet round.

TIP

Raised stitches are worked around the post or stem of the stitch from the previous round and not into the top of the stitch. When worked as in this pattern, alternating front and back post stitches, they result in a rib effect at the brim of the hat.

Baby's Pompom Hat

This very cute hat is made with super soft merino wool so it will not irritate delicate skin. It's such an easy hat to crochet that it can be made over one evening.

SKILL RATING: ● ◐ ◐

YARN AND MATERIALS

Debbie Bliss Rialto DK (100% merino wool, approx. 105m/115yd per 50g/1¾oz ball) DK (light worsted) weight yarn
1 ball each of shades:
009 Apple (green) (A)
002 Ecru (off-white) (B)

3.5mm (US size E/4) crochet hook

Yarn sewing needle

SIZE

To fit age (approx.) 12–36 months

FINISHED MEASUREMENTS

45–50cm (18–20in) around, 17.5cm (7in) from crown to edge

TENSION

Tension is not critical on this project.

ABBREVIATIONS

approx.	approximately
ch	chain
dc	double crochet
htr	half treble
rep	repeat
ss	slip stitch
st(s)	stitch(es)
yrh	yarn round hook

SPECIAL ABBREVIATIONS

CL (cluster): yrh, insert hook in st, yrh, pull yarn through, yrh, insert hook in same st, yrh, pull yarn through, yrh, insert hook in same st, yrh, pull yarn through, yrh (7 loops on hook), pull yarn through all 7 loops on hook, yrh, make 1ch

htr2tog (half treble 2 stitches together): [yrh, insert hook in next st, yrh, pull yarn through] twice (5 loops on hook), yrh, pull through all 5 loops on hook

HAT

Using A, make 76ch.
Row 1: 1dc in next ch from hook, 1dc in each ch to end.
Rows 2–3: 1ch, 1dc in each st to end.
Row 4: 1ch, 1dc in each of next 5 sts, 2dc in next st, *1dc in each of next 4 sts, 2dc in next st; rep from * to last 5 sts, 1dc in each of next 5 sts. *(90 sts)*
Row 5: 1dc in each st to end. *(90 sts)*
Change to B.
Rows 6–7: 1dc in each st. *(90 sts)*
Change to A.
Rows 8–9: 1dc in each st. *(90 sts)*
Change to B.
Row 10: 3ch, *1CL in next st, miss 1 st; rep from * to last st, 1htr.
Change to A.
Rows 11–12: 2ch, 1htr in each st to end.
Row 13: 2ch, *1htr in each of next 7 sts, htr2tog; rep from * to end. *(80 sts)*
Change to B.
Row 14: 3ch, miss first st, *1CL in next st, miss 1 st; rep from * to last st, 1htr.
Change to A.
Row 15: 1ch, 1dc in each st to end.
Row 16: 2ch, *1htr in each of next 6 sts, htr2tog; rep from * to end. *(70 sts)*
Row 17: 2ch, *1htr in each st to end.
Row 18: 2ch, *1htr in each of next 5 sts, htr2tog; rep from * to end. *(60 sts)*
Row 19: 2ch, *1htr in each st to end.
Row 20: 2ch, *1htr in each of next 4 sts, htr2tog; rep from * to end. *(50 sts)*

Row 21: Rep Row 19.
Row 22: 2ch, htr2tog, *1htr in each of next 3 sts, htr2tog; rep from * to end. *(40 sts)*
Row 23: 2ch, *1htr in each of next 2 sts, htr2tog; rep from * to end. *(30 sts)*
Row 24: 2ch, *htr2tog, 1htr in next st; rep from * to end. *(20 sts)*
Fasten off leaving a long tail approx. 30cm (12in).

FINISHING

Sew in the ends.

Thread the long yarn tail into a yarn sewing needle and make a running stitch around the last row. Pull the yarn tight and gather the top together, then sew in securely.

Oversew the seam together.

Using A and B together, make a small pompom (see page 110). Fluff the pompom into shape and sew onto the top of the hat.

Peaked Toddler Hat

The little peak on this hat makes it a very cute version of the traditional beanie. The design is great for a girl or a boy.

SKILL RATING: ● ● ●

YARN AND MATERIALS

Debbie Bliss Cashmerino Aran
(55% merino wool/33% microfibre/
12% cashmere, approx. 90m/98yd
per 50g/1¾oz ball) Aran (worsted)
weight yarn
    1 ball each of shades:
    076 Willow (light green) (A)
    064 Cowslip (light orange) (B)

3.5mm (US size E/4) crochet hook

Yarn sewing needle

SIZE

To fit age 18–36 months

TENSION

Tension is not critical on this project.

ABBREVIATIONS

approx.	approximately
beg	beginning
ch	chain
ch sp	chain space
dc	double crochet
dc2tog	double crochet 2 stitches together
htr	half treble
rep	repeat
RS	right side
ss	slip stitch
st(s)	stitch(es)
tr	treble

SPECIAL ABBREVIATION

htr2tog (half treble 2 stitches together):
[yrh, insert hook in next st, yrh, pull yarn
through] twice (5 loops on hook), yrh,
pull through all 5 loops on hook

HAT

Using A, make 80ch, join with a ss in
first ch to make a ring.
Round 1: 2ch, 1htr in each ch, join
with a ss in first 2-ch.
Rounds 2–4: 2ch, 1htr in each st, join
with a ss in first 2-ch.
Round 5: 1ch, 1dc in each st, join
with a ss in first ch.
Round 6: 1ch, *1dc in each of next
18 sts, dc2tog; rep from * to end, join
with a ss in first ch.
Round 7: Rep Round 5.
Round 8: 2ch, 1htr in each st, join
with a ss in first 2-ch.
Round 9: 2ch, *1htr in each of next
17 sts, htr2tog; rep from * to end, join
with a ss in first 2-ch.
Rounds 10–11: Rep Round 8.
(68 sts)
Round 12: 1ch, 1dc in each of next
6 sts, *dc2tog, 1dc in next 6 sts; rep
from * to end, join with a ss in first ch.
(60 sts)
Rounds 13–14: Rep Round 5.
Round 15: 2ch, 1htr in each of next
4 sts, htr2tog; rep from * to end, join
with a ss in first 2-ch.
Round 16: Rep Round 8.
Round 17: 2ch, 1htr in each of next
3 sts, htr2tog; rep from * to end, join
with a ss in first 2-ch.
Round 18: 2ch, *1htr in each of next
2 sts, htr2tog; rep from * to last 3 sts,
1htr, htr2tog, join with a ss in first
2-ch.

Round 19: 2ch, *1htr in next st,
htr2tog; rep from * to end, join with a
ss in first 2-ch.
Round 20: 2ch, *1htr in each st, join
with a ss in first 2-ch.
Round 21: 2ch, *htr2tog; rep from *
to end, join with a ss in first 2-ch.
Fasten off.

HEAD PEAK:

With RS of hat facing, count 21 sts
from beg of first round to left. Join
yarn in 22nd st, work 1dc in each of
next 38 sts. Turn.
Rows 1–3: Miss 1 st, 1dc in each st
to last 2 sts, miss 1 st, 1dc in last st.
Row 4: Dc2tog twice, 1dc in each st
to last 4 sts, dc2tog twice.
Row 5: Miss 1 st, 1dc in each st to
last 2 sts, miss 1 st, 1dc in last st.
Row 6: Miss 1 st, dc2tog, 1dc in
each st to last 4 sts, dc2tog, miss
1 st, 1dc in last st.
Row 7: Miss 1 st, 1dc in each st to
last 2 sts, miss 1 st, 1dc in last st.
Row 8: Rep Row 7 until 14 sts
remain.
Fasten off, leaving a long tail for
sewing on later.

FLOWER

Using B, make 35ch.

Row 1: 1tr in fifth ch from hook, *1ch, miss 1 ch, [1tr, 1ch, 1tr] in next ch; rep from * to end.

Row 2: 3ch, 5tr in first ch sp, *1dc in next ch sp, 6tr in next ch sp; rep from *, ending with 6tr in last ch sp. *(16 shells)*

Fasten off, leaving a long tail for sewing flower together.

FINISHING

To finish the peak, thread the yarn tail into a yarn sewing needle, turn the last two double crochet rows inward and sew them to the inside of the peak to make a firm edge.

FLOWER:

To finish the flower, thread the needle with the yarn tail and weave down the side of the shell to the bottom. Roll the first shell tightly to form the centre bud. Stitch at the base of the shell with two stitches to hold it in place, then roll the remaining strip around the bud to form the rose, securing as you roll by stitching through the layers of chains at the bottom of the rose. Sew the rose onto the side of the hat.

Pompom Beanie Hats

These hats can be made in an evening and make great gifts. You'll need a stitch marker for this project, but if you don't have one, just use a short length of contrasting yarn. If making the hat for yourself, try it on for size as you go and either add more rows or omit Round 16 (17:17) to make it shorter.

SKILL RATING: ● ● ●

YARN AND MATERIALS

Debbie Bliss Paloma (60% alpaca/ 40% wool, approx. 65m/71yd per 50g/1¾oz hank) super-chunky (super-bulky) weight yarn

ONE-COLOUR RED HAT:

2(**3**:3) hanks of shade 015 Ruby (red) (MC)
1 hank of shade 024 Silver (grey) (CC)

ONE-COLOUR GREY HAT:

2(**3**:3) hanks of shade 024 Silver (grey) (MC)
1 hank of shade 015 Ruby (red) (CC)

TWO-COLOUR WHITE HAT
WITH BLUE BRIM:

2 hanks of shade 001 Ecru (white) (MC)
2 hanks of shade 044 Robin Egg (pale blue) (CC)

TWO-COLOUR BLUE HAT
WITH GREEN BRIM:

2 hanks of shade 044 Robin Egg (pale blue) (MC)
2 hanks of shade 026 Lime (light green) (CC)

6mm (US size J/10) crochet hook

Yarn sewing needle

FINISHED MEASUREMENTS

Small: Approx. 50cm (20in) around, 19cm (7½in) from crown to folded edge of brim
Medium: Approx. 55cm (22in) around, 20cm (7¾in) from crown to folded edge of brim
Large: Approx. 60cm (24in) around, 20cm (7¾in) from crown to folded edge of brim

TENSION

11 sts x 9 rows over a 10cm (4in) square working half treble, using a 6mm (US size J/10) hook and Debbie Bliss Paloma.

ABBREVIATIONS

approx. approximately
beg begin(ning)
CC contrast colour
ch chain
cont continue
htr half treble
MC main colour
rep repeat
RS right side
ss slip stitch
st(s) stitch(es)
tr treble
WS wrong side
yrh yarn round hook

SPECIAL ABBREVIATIONS

rt/rf (raised treble round front): yrh, insert hook from front and around post (stem) of next tr from right to left, yrh, pull yarn through work, [yrh, pull yarn through first 2 loops on hook] twice

rt/rb (raised treble round back): yrh, insert hook from back and around post (stem) of next tr from right to left, yrh, pull yarn through work, [yrh, pull yarn through first 2 loops on hook] twice

HAT

Using MC, beg hat at centre top as follows:

Round 1 (RS): Make 2ch, 10htr in 2nd ch from hook. *(10 htr)*

Mark beg of each round and cont in rounds with RS always facing you.

Round 2: Miss 2-ch at beg of round, 2htr in each htr to end. *(20 htr)*

Remember to keep moving marker to mark beg of each round.

Round 3: *1htr in next htr, 2htr in next htr; rep from * to end. *(30 htr)*

LARGE SIZE ONLY:

Round –:–:4: *1htr in each of next 4 htr, 2htr in next htr; rep from * to end. *(–:–:36 htr)*

ALL SIZES:

Round 4:4:5: *1htr in each of next 5 htr, 2htr in next htr; rep from * to end. *(35:**35**:42 htr)*

Round 5:5:6: *1htr in each of next 6 htr, 2htr in next htr; rep from * to end. *(40:**40**:48 htr)*

Round 6:6:7: *1htr in each of next 7 htr, 2htr in next htr; rep from * to end. *(45:**45**:54 htr)*

Round 7:7:8: *1htr in each of next 8 htr, 2htr in next htr; rep from * to end. *(50:**50**:60 htr)*

MEDIUM SIZE ONLY:

Round –:8:–: *1htr in each of next 9 htr, 2htr in next htr; rep from * to end. *(–:**55**:– htr)*

ALL SIZES:

Rounds 8:9:9–16:17:17: 1htr in each htr to end. *(50:**55**:60 htr)*

BRIM:

For one-colour hat, cont in MC. For two-colour hat, cut off MC, join CC for next round.

Brim round 1: 1htr in each htr to end.

Keep RS of hat facing while working brim: brim is later turned up, so WS of brim will be facing you as you work it.

Brim round 2: 1rt/rf (round front) around each htr to end.

Brim rounds 3, 4 and 5: 1 rt/rb (round back) around each raised tr to end.

Brim round 6: 1rt/rb around each raised tr to last st, join with a ss around last st.

Fasten off.

There will be 4 raised 'ribs' on the WS of the brim.

Turn brim up so RS of brim is showing on RS of hat.

FINISHING

Using a yarn sewing needle, sew in all yarn ends – as you do this, neaten the join at the last brim stitch and the ring at the centre of the top of the hat.

Press the brim carefully using a damp cloth, ensuring that it's neat and straight.

POMPOM:

Using CC, make one large pompom with the remaining yarn (see page 110). Trim the pompom to approx. 7.5cm (3in) diameter and then sew it to the top of the hat.

TIPS

The hat is started at the centre top and worked downward in a spiral towards the brim edge.

Mark the beginning (and end) of each round by inserting a stitch marker in the loop on the hook at the beginning of each round of the hat section, and in front of the raised treble on the brim section.

Instructions for the small size come first and those for the medium and large sizes follow; if there is only one figure, it applies to all sizes.

Turban Headband

A really quick and easy project, this headband is ideal for beginners. It can be made in a couple of hours, keeps you warm and is a lot less bulky than a thick hat.

SKILL RATING: ● ● ●

YARN AND MATERIALS

Debbie Bliss Rialto DK (100% merino wool, approx. 105m/115yd per 50g/1¾oz ball) DK (light worsted) weight yarn
    2 balls of shade 020 Teal
    (dark turquoise)

4mm (US size G/6) crochet hook

Yarn sewing needle

SIZE

One size

FINISHED MEASUREMENTS

49 x 9.5cm (19¼ x 3¾in)

TENSION

16 sts x 10 rows over 10cm (4in) square working half treble, using a 4mm (US size G/6) hook and Debbie Bliss Rialto DK.

ABBREVIATIONS

approx. approximately
ch chain
htr half treble
rep repeat
RS right side
ss slip stitch
st(s) stitch(es)
WS wrong side

HEADBAND

Make 17ch.
Row 1: 1htr in 2nd ch from hook, 1htr in each ch to end. *(15 sts)*
Row 2: 2ch, 1htr in each st to end.
Rep Row 2 until work measures approx. 49cm (19¼in) or to fit around head.
Fasten off.

FRONT TIE

Make 10ch.
Row 1: 1htr in 2nd ch from hook. *(9 sts)*
Row 2: 2ch, 1htr in each st to end.
Rep Row 2 until work measures approx. 9cm (3½in).
Fasten off.

FINISHING

Fold the headband in half with RS together, so the short ends meet. Join the ends together with a double crochet seam. Turn RS out.

Wrap the tie around the headband and join the seam ends of tie with a double crochet seam, making sure the seam is on the WS of the headband.

Ribbon Baby Hat

This is a perfect first baby hat. It's so easy to make and the ribbon and flower add a delicate and stylish look.

SKILL RATING:

YARN AND MATERIALS

Debbie Bliss Baby Cashmerino (55% wool/33% acrylic/12% cashmere, approx. 125m/137yd per 50g/1¾oz ball) 4ply (sport) weight yarn
    1 ball of shade 101 Ecru (off-white) (A)
    Small amount of shade 608 Pale Lilac (lilac) (B)
    Small amount of shade 010 Lilac (purple) (C)

3mm (US size D/3) crochet hook

Yarn sewing needle

Approx. 50cm (20in) of 1cm (½in) wide lilac ribbon

SIZE

To fit newborn baby

FINISHED MEASUREMENT

37.5cm (15in) around

TENSION

24 sts x 15 rows over a 10cm (4in) square working pattern, using a 3mm (US size D/3) hook and Debbie Bliss Baby Cashmerino.

ABBREVIATIONS

approx. approximately
ch chain
ch sp chain space
dc double crochet
htr half treble
rep repeat
ss slip stitch
st(s) stitch(es)
tr treble

HAT

Using A, make 4ch, ss in first ch to form a ring.

Round 1: 5ch, *1tr, 2ch in ring; rep from * 4 more times, ss in third ch of 5-ch, ss in fourth ch of same 5-ch.

Round 2: 5ch, *1tr in first ch sp, 2ch, *[1tr, 2ch, 1tr] in next ch sp; rep from * to end, ss in third ch of first 5-ch, ss in fourth ch of same 5-ch.

Round 3: 5ch, 1tr in first ch sp, *2ch, 1tr in next ch sp, 2ch, [1tr, 2ch, 1tr] in next ch sp; rep from * to end, ss in third ch of 5-ch, ss in fourth ch of same 5-ch.

Round 4: 5ch, 1tr in first ch sp, *2ch, 1tr in next ch sp, 2ch, 1tr in next ch sp, 2ch, [1tr, 2ch, 1tr] in next ch sp; rep from * to end, ss in third ch of 5-ch, ss in fourth ch of same 5-ch.

Round 5: 5ch, 1tr in first ch sp, *2ch, 1tr in next ch sp, 2ch, 1tr in next ch sp, 2ch, 1tr in next ch sp, 2ch, [1tr, 2ch, 1tr] in next ch sp; rep from * to end, ss in third ch of 5-ch, ss in fourth ch of same 5-ch.

Round 6: 5ch, 1tr in first ch sp, *2ch, 1tr in next ch sp, 2ch, 1tr in next ch sp, 2ch, 1tr in next ch sp, 2ch, 1tr in next ch sp, 2ch, [1tr, 2ch, 1tr] in next ch sp; rep from * to end, ss in third ch of 5-ch, ss in fourth ch of same 5-ch.

Rounds 7–16: 5ch, 1tr, 1ch in each ch sp around, ss in third ch of 5-ch, ss in fourth ch of same 5-ch. *(36 sts)*

Round 17: 1ch, *2dc in next ch sp, 1dc in next ch sp, 3ch, ss in first ch, 1dc in same ch sp, 2dc in next ch sp, 3ch, ss in first ch; rep from * to end, ss in first ch to join round.
Fasten off.

FLOWER

Using B, make 4ch, ss in first ch to make a ring.

Round 1: [3ch, 1dc in middle of 4-ch] 5 times (5 holes for petals), ss in first ch.

Round 2: [1dc, 1htr, 2tr, 1htr, 1dc] in each ch sp, ss in base of first 3-ch from previous round.
Change to C.

Round 3: [Place hook through centre hole from front to back and back through middle hole of any petal, make 1dc, 3ch] 5 times.

Round 4: [1dc, 1tr, 1dc] in each ch sp, ss in base of first dc.
Fasten off.

FINISHING

Sew in any ends.

Weave the ribbon around the holes in the stitches. Sew the ends of the ribbon together to attach.

Stitch the flower to the hat.

CHAPTER 2
SIMPLE SCARVES AND WRAPS

Chunky Patchwork Scarf

An outrageously long, chunky, bright scarf for instant style!

YARN AND MATERIALS

Debbie Bliss Cashmerino Aran
(55% merino wool/33% microfibre/
12% cashmere, approx. 90m/98yd
per 50g/1¾oz ball) Aran (worsted)
weight yarn

 4 balls of shade 300 Black (MC)
 2 balls of shade 101 Ecru (off-white)
 1 ball each of shades:
 054 Crimson (red)
 202 Silver (pale blue)
 082 Duck Egg (blue-green)
 048 Burnt Orange (orange)
 073 Coral (pink)
 064 Cowslip (yellow)
 027 Oatmeal (pale blue)
 502 Lime (green)
 084 Lilac
 205 Denim (blue)

5mm (US size H/8) crochet hook

Yarn sewing needle

FINISHED MEASUREMENTS

Approx. 30 x 300cm (12 x 118in)

TENSION

Each square measures approx. 15cm
(6in), using a 5mm (US size H/8) hook
and Debbie Bliss Cashmerino Aran.

ABBREVIATIONS

approx.	approximately
ch	chain
cont	continu(e)(ing)
dc	double crochet
MC	main colour
rep	repeat
RS	right side
sp(s)	space(s)
ss	slip stitch
st(s)	stitch(es)
tr	treble

SQUARE

(make 40)
Using first colour, make 4ch, join with a ss to form a ring.
Round 1: 3ch, 2tr in ring, 2ch, *[3tr, 2ch] in ring; rep from * twice more (4 tr groups), join with a ss in top of first 3-ch.
Fasten off first colour.
With RS facing, join 2nd colour in any 2-ch sp.
Round 2: 3ch, [2tr, 2ch, 3tr] in same ch sp, *1ch, [3tr, 2ch, 3tr] in next ch sp; rep from * twice more, 1ch, join with a ss in top of first 3-ch.
Fasten off 2nd colour.
With RS facing, join 3rd colour in next 2-ch sp (corner).
Round 3: 3ch, [2tr, 2ch, 3tr] in same ch sp, *1ch, 3tr in next ch sp, 1ch, [3tr, 2ch, 3tr] in next ch sp (corner); rep from * twice more, 1ch, 3tr in next ch sp, 1ch, join with a ss in top of first 3-ch.
Fasten off 3rd colour.
With RS facing, join 4th colour in next 2-ch sp (corner).
Round 4: 3ch, [2tr, 2ch, 3tr] in same ch sp, *[1ch, 3tr in next ch sp] twice, 1ch, [3tr, 2ch, 3tr] in next ch sp (corner); rep from * twice more, [1ch, 3tr in next ch sp] twice, 1ch, join with a ss in top of first 3-ch.
Fasten off 4th colour.
With RS facing, join MC in next 2-ch sp (corner).
Round 5: 3ch, [2tr, 2ch, 3tr] in same ch sp (corner), *[1ch, 3tr in next ch sp] 3 times in each of next 3 ch sps, 1ch, [3tr, 2ch, 3tr] in next ch sp (corner); rep from * twice more, [1ch, 3tr in next ch sp] 3 times, 1ch, join with ss in top of first 3-ch.
Fasten off, sew in ends.

FINISHING

Join the squares together in 20 rows of two, using a double crochet seam. Sew in the ends.

Note: Use four colours at random in Rounds 1, 2, 3 and 4, occasionally using same colour for Rounds 2 and 4, 1 and 4, or 2 and 3. Always use MC in Round 5.

Textured Neckerchief

I've used a combination of different thickness yarns here, chosen for colour and texture. And I've added the simplest edging – but feel free to add any edging you like.

SKILL RATING: ● ● ●

YARN AND MATERIALS

Debbie Bliss Rialto DK (100% merino wool, approx. 105m/115yd per 50g/1¾oz ball) DK (light worsted) weight yarn
    1 ball of shade 002 Ecru (off-white) (MC)
    ¼ ball each of shades:
    057 Banana (yellow)
    072 Ocean (dark blue)
    019 Duck Egg (light blue)
    017 Navy (dark blue)

Debbie Bliss Cashmerino Aran (55% merino wool/33% acrylic/12% cashmere, approx. 90m/98yd per 50g/1¾oz ball) Aran (worsted) weight yarn
    ¼ ball of shade 073 Coral (orange)

Lamana Piura (100% alpaca, approx. 400m/437yd per 50g/1¾oz ball) laceweight yarn
    ½ ball each of shades:
    045 Karibikblau/Caribbean Blue (turquoise)
    039 Koralle/Coral (orange)
    038 Lind/Linden Green (pale green)
    033 Karmin (pink)
    015 Chili (red)

Rico Luxury Magic Mohair (34% polyester/28% mohair/ 28% polyamide/10% wool, approx. 200m/219yd per 50g/1¾oz ball) Aran (worsted) weight yarn
    ¼ ball of shade 003 Silver

3.5mm (US size E/4) crochet hook

Yarn sewing needle

FINISHED MEASUREMENTS

36cm (14in) deep x 45cm (17¾in) across top edge

TENSION

17 sts over 10cm (4in) working half treble, using a 3.5mm (US size E/4) hook; row tension is not critical on this project.

ABBREVIATIONS

approx.	approximately
ch	chain
cont	continu(e)(ing)
dc	double crochet
dtr	double treble
htr	half treble
MC	main colour
rep	repeat
RS	right side
ss	slip stitch
st(s)	stitch(es)
tch	turning chain
tr	treble
WS	wrong side

NECKERCHIEF

Using first colour, make 2ch, 2dc in 2nd ch from hook. *(2 sts)*
Row 1: 1ch, 2dc in each st. *(4 sts)*
Row 2 (WS): 1ch, 2dc in first st, 1dc in each of next 2 sts, 2dc in last st.
Cont in stripes of 1, 2 or 3 rows of htr, using colours randomly.
Next row: 2ch, 1htr in first st, 1htr in each st to last st, 2htr in top of tch.
Rep last row until work measures 30cm (11¾in), ending with a RS row.
Fasten off.

TOP EDGING:

Using MC, make 90ch (first tie).
Row 1 (WS): Join ch to right-hand corner of top edge (first tie), make 1dc in each st along top, make 90ch (2nd tie).
Row 2 (RS): 1dc in 2nd ch from hook and in each ch to top edge, 1dc in each st along top edge, 1dc in each ch to end of second tie.
Row 3 (WS): 1ch, 1dc in first st, *2ch, miss next 2 sts, 1dc in next st; rep from * to end.
Row 4 (RS): 1ch, *[1dc, 1ch, 1htr, 1ch, 1tr, 1ch, 1dtr, 1ch] in next ch loop, 1dtr in next dc, 1ch, [1dtr, 1ch, 1tr, 1ch, 1htr, 1ch, 1dc] in next loop, 1dc in next dc; rep from * to end.
Fasten off.

SIDE EDGING:

Row 1: With WS facing, join MC at top left edge. Work dc along length to tip, 3dc in tip, work dc along 2nd side to top edge.

Row 2 (RS): 1ch, 1dc in each st along first side, 3dc in tip, 1dc in each st along 2nd side.

Row 3 (WS): 1ch, 1dc in first st, *2ch, miss next 2 sts, 1dc in next st; rep from * to end.

Row 4 (RS): 1ch, * [1dc, 1ch, 1htr, 1ch, 1tr, 1ch, 1dtr, 1ch] in next ch loop, 1dtr in next dc, 1ch, [1dtr, 1ch, 1tr, 1ch, 1htr, 1ch, 1dc] in next loop, 1dc in next dc; rep from * to end.

Fasten off.

FINISHING

Sew in all ends and block.

Tweedy Scarf

A really lovely stitch that shows off these bright colours well.
The tassels give the edges a bit of zing and swish.

SKILL RATING: ● ● ◐

YARN AND MATERIALS

Debbie Bliss Rialto DK (100% merino wool, approx. 105m/115yd per 50g/1¾oz ball) DK (light worsted) weight yarn
  1 ball each of shades:
  072 Ocean (blue) (A)
  012 Scarlet (red) (B)
  066 Vintage Pink (pink) (C)
  005 Chocolate (brown) (D)
  019 Duck Egg (blue-green) (E)
  002 Ecru (off-white) (F)
  099 Mustard (yellow) (G)

4mm (US size G/6) crochet hook

Yarn sewing needle

FINISHED MEASUREMENTS

Approx. 12.5 x 160cm (5 x 63in)

TENSION

25 sts x 21 rows over a 10cm (4in) square working tweed stitch, using a 4mm (US size G/6) hook and Debbie Bliss Rialto DK.

ABBREVIATIONS

approx.	approximately
ch	chain
ch sp	chain space
dc	double crochet
rep	repeat
ss	slip stitch
st(s)	stitch(es)

SCARF

Using A, make 34ch.
Row 1: 1dc in second ch from hook, 1dc in each ch to end. *(33 sts)*
Cut yarn, do not fasten off.
Row 2: Join B, 1ch, 1dc in each of first 2 sts, *1ch, miss next st, 1dc in next st; rep from * to last st, ending row with 1dc in last st.
Cut yarn, do not fasten off.
Row 3: Join C, 1ch, 1dc in first st, *1ch, 1dc in next ch sp; rep from * to last 2 sts, 1ch, miss next st, 1dc in last st.
Cut yarn, do not fasten off.
Row 4: Join D, 1ch, 1dc in first st, 1dc in first ch sp, *1ch, 1dc in next ch sp; rep from * to last st, 1dc in last dc.
Cut yarn, do not fasten off.
Rep Rows 3 and 4, using the following colour sequence: E, F, G, A, B, C, D, until scarf measures approx. 160cm (63in), ending with row using A.
Do not cut yarn.
Last row: 1ch, 1dc in each dc and in each ch sp to end. Fasten off.

FINISHING

Sew in the ends.

TASSELS:
Using B, cut sixty 25.5cm (10in) lengths of yarn, to make 30 tassels in all (15 for each end of the scarf). Fold two strands of yarn in half to make each tassel. Attach the first tassel (see page 110) to the first chain stitch at one end of the scarf, then attach one tassel in every alternate chain stitch, ending with one tassel in the end chain stitch. Attach the remaining 15 tassels to the other end of the scarf.

Chunky Scarf

This is a very easy stitch, but it takes some concentration because the stitches are hard to see. The yarn is thick and soft so, even though it's a wide scarf, it scrunches around the neck very cosily.

SKILL RATING: ● ● ●

YARN AND MATERIALS

Berroco Ultra Alpaca Chunky (50% alpaca/50% wool, approx. 120m/131yd per 100g/3½oz ball) chunky (bulky) weight yarn
   3 balls of shade 07201 Winter White (off-white)

10mm (US size N/15) crochet hook

Yarn sewing needle

FINISHED MEASUREMENTS

Approx. 26.5 x 229cm (10½ x 90in), including edging

TENSION

7 sts x 7 rows over a 10cm (4in) square working double crochet, using a 10mm (US size N/15) hook and Berroco Ultra Alpaca Chunky.

ABBREVIATIONS

approx. approximately
ch chain
dc double crochet
rep repeat
ss slip stitch
st(s) stitch(es)
tr treble
yrh yarn round hook

SPECIAL ABBREVIATION

3trCL (3-treble cluster): *yrh, insert hook in st or sp, yrh, pull yarn through, yrh, pull through first 2 loops on hook, rep from * twice more (4 loops on hook), yrh, pull yarn through all 4 loops on hook

SCARF

Make 18ch.
Row 1: 1dc in second ch from hook, 1dc in each ch to end. *(17 sts)*
Row 2: 1ch, 1dc in each st to end. *(17 sts)*
Rep Row 2 until work measures approx. 218cm (86in).
Do not fasten off.
Turn work and start next row of edging along last row worked of scarf.

EDGING SIDE 1:
*Make 6ch, 3trCL in third ch from hook, ss in next ch, 2ch, miss 1 st, 1dc in next st; rep from * to end. *(8 x 3trCL)*
Fasten off.

EDGING SIDE 2:
Join yarn in first ch of Row 1 and rep from * of edging side 1.
Fasten off.

FINISHING

Sew in all ends.

Skinny Scarf

A long skinny scarf that really showcases the gorgeous colours of these yarns, which go with everything. Play around with the colours to show off your individuality.

SKILL RATING: ● ● ●

YARN AND MATERIALS

Debbie Bliss Baby Cashmerino (55% wool/33% acrylic/12% cashmere, approx. 125m/137yd per 50g/1¾oz ball) 4ply (sport) weight yarn
    1 ball each of shades:
    018 Citrus (green) (A)
    012 Silver (pale grey) (D)
    91 Acid Yellow (yellow) (E)
    204 Baby Blue (pale blue) (G)
    101 Ecru (off-white) (H)

Cascade 220 Sport (100% wool, approx. 150m/164yd per 50g/1¾oz ball) 4ply (sport) weight yarn
    1 ball each of shades:
    8891 Cyan Blue (bright blue) (B)
    9682 Desert Flower (peach) (C)
    1016 Bordeaux (purple) (F)

4mm (US size G/6) crochet hook

Yarn sewing needle

FINISHED MEASUREMENTS

Approx. 11.5 x 239cm (4½ x 94in)

TENSION

20 sts x 20 rows over a 10cm (4in) square working double crochet, using a 4mm (US size G/6) hook and Debbie Bliss Baby Cashmerino.

ABBREVIATIONS

approx. approximately
ch chain
cont continue
dc double crochet
rep repeat
st(s) stitch(es)

SCARF

Using B, make 23ch.
Row 1: 1dc in second ch from hook, 1dc in each ch to end. *(22 sts)*
Rows 2–4: 1ch, 1dc in each st to end. *(22 sts)*
Cut yarn, do not fasten off.
Next 4 rows: Join A, rep Row 2. Cut yarn, do not fasten off.
Next 4 rows: Join G, rep Row 2. Cut yarn, do not fasten off.
Next 32 rows: Join C, rep Row 2. Cut yarn, do not fasten off.
Next 32 rows: Join E, rep Row 2. Cut yarn, do not fasten off.
Next 4 rows: Join F, rep Row 2. Cut yarn, do not fasten off.
Next 4 rows: Join H, rep Row 2. Cut yarn, do not fasten off.
Next 4 rows: Join A, rep Row 2. Cut yarn, do not fasten off.
Next 32 rows: Join B, rep Row 2. Cut yarn, do not fasten off.
Next 32 rows: Join G, rep Row 2. Cut yarn, do not fasten off.
Next 4 rows: Join C, rep Row 2. Cut yarn, do not fasten off.
Next 4 rows: Join E, rep Row 2. Cut yarn, do not fasten off.
Next 4 rows: Join H, rep Row 2. Cut yarn, do not fasten off.
Next 64 rows: Join D, rep Row 2. Cut yarn, do not fasten off.
Next 64 rows: Join H, rep Row 2. Cut yarn, do not fasten off.

Next 4 rows: Join G, rep Row 2. Cut yarn, do not fasten off.
Next 4 rows: Join B, rep Row 2. Cut yarn, do not fasten off.
Next 4 rows: Join E, rep Row 2. Cut yarn, do not fasten off.
Next 32 rows: Join C, rep Row 2. Cut yarn, do not fasten off.
Next 32 rows: Join G, rep Row 2. Cut yarn, do not fasten off.
Next 4 rows: Join A, rep Row 2. Cut yarn, do not fasten off.
Next 4 rows: Join D, rep Row 2. Cut yarn, do not fasten off.
Next 4 rows: Join F, rep Row 2. Cut yarn, do not fasten off.
Next 32 rows: Join E, rep Row 2. Cut yarn, do not fasten off.
Next 32 rows: Join D, rep Row 2. Cut yarn, do not fasten off.
Next 4 rows: Join C, rep Row 2. Cut yarn, do not fasten off.
Next 4 rows: Join B, rep Row 2. Cut yarn, do not fasten off.
Next 4 rows: Join A, rep Row 2. Fasten off.

FINISHING

Sew in all ends.

Tasselled Baby Poncho

This is a really popular and classic poncho, one of the first crochet projects I ever made. The cotton yarn is very soft and non-itchy – perfect for babies.

YARN AND MATERIALS

Rico Essentials Cotton DK
(100% cotton, approx. 130m/142yd
per 50g/1¾oz ball) DK (light worsted)
weight yarn
> 1:**1** ball of shade 086 Pistachio
> (green) (A)
> 2:**3** balls of shade 060 Saffron
> (pale yellow) (B)
> 1:**1** ball of shade 057 Lotus
> (bright pink) (C)

3.5mm (US size E/4) crochet hook

Yarn sewing needle

SIZE

Small: To fit age 6–12 months
Medium: To fit age 12–18 months

FINISHED MEASUREMENTS

Small: 30cm (12in) long, 22.5cm (9in)
side length
Medium: 37.5cm (15in) long, 30cm
(12in) side length

TENSION

5 patt x 9 rows over a 10cm (4in)
square, using a 3.5mm (US size E/4)
hook and Rico Essentials Cotton DK.

ABBREVIATIONS

approx.	approximately
ch	chain
ch sp	chain space
dc	double crochet
inc	increase
patt	pattern
rep	repeat
ss	slip stitch
st(s)	stitch(es)
tr	treble

PONCHO

Using A, make 72:**88**ch, join with a ss to form a ring.
Round 1: 1ch, 1dc in each ch to end, ss in first ch using B. *(72:**88** sts)*
Fasten off A.
Round 2: 3ch, 1tr in each of next 2 sts, 1ch, miss 1 st, *1tr in each of next 3 sts, 1ch, miss 1 st; rep from * to end, join with a ss in top of first 3-ch.
Round 3: Ss in each of next 2 sts, ss in next ch sp, 3ch, [2tr, 1ch, 3tr] in same ch sp, *1ch, 3tr in next ch sp; rep from * 7:**9** times more, 1ch [3tr, 1ch, 3tr] in next ch sp, 1ch, 3tr in next ch sp; rep from * 7:**9** times more, 1ch, ss in top of first 3-tr.
Round 4: Ss in each of next 2 sts, ss in next ch sp, 3ch, [2tr, 1ch, 3tr] in same ch sp *1ch, 3tr in next ch sp; rep from * to next inc group from previous round, 1ch [3tr, 1ch, 3tr] in next ch sp (middle of inc group), 1ch, 3tr in next ch sp; rep from * to end of round, 1ch, ss in top of first 3-tr.
Rep Round 4 until 20:**26** rows in total have been worked (or make to required length).
Fasten off.

FINISHING

Sew in ends.

TASSELS:

Using C, make approx. 5cm (2in) tassels by wrapping the yarn around four fingers four times for each tassel. Remove from the fingers and cut the yarn at the bottom. Add the tassels as explained on page 110, inserting one into each space along the outer edge.

Wave and Chevron Chunky Scarf

This lovely pattern resembles a Fair Isle stitch in knitting. These colours look great together, but experiment with whatever colours suit you.

YARN AND MATERIALS

Cascade 220 (100% wool, approx. 200m/219yd per 100g/3½oz ball) Aran (worsted) weight yarn
  2 balls of shade 9484 Stratosphere (dark blue) (A)
  1 ball each of shades:
  8414 Bright Red (red) (B)
  7827 Goldenrod (yellow) (C)
  8555 Black (D)

4.5mm (US size G/7) crochet hook

Yarn sewing needle

FINISHED MEASUREMENTS

Approx. 235 x 19cm (92½ x 7½in)

TENSION

14 sts x 11 rows over a 10cm (4in) square working wave and chevron stitch pattern, using a 4.5mm (US size G/7) hook and Cascade 220.

ABBREVIATIONS

approx.	approximately
beg	beginning
ch	chain
cont	continu(e)(ing)
dc	double crochet
dc2tog	double crochet 2 stitches together
dtr	double treble
foll	following
htr	half treble
rep	repeat
patt	pattern
RS	right side
ss	slip stitch
st(s)	stitch(es)
tr	treble
yrh	yarn round hook

SPECIAL ABBREVIATIONS

dc3tog (double crochet 3 stitches together): [insert hook in next st, yrh, pull yarn through] 3 times, yrh, pull through all 4 loops on hook

dtr2tog (double treble 2 stitches together): *yrh twice, insert hook in next st, yrh, pull yarn through, [yrh, pull through first 2 loops on hook] twice; rep from * once more, yrh, pull through all 3 loops on hook

dtr3tog (double treble 3 stitches together): *yrh twice, insert hook in next st, yrh, pull yarn through, [yrh, pull through first 2 loops on hook] twice; rep from * twice more, yrh, pull through all 4 loops on hook

SCARF

Using A, make 25ch.
Row 1 (RS): 1dc in 2nd ch from hook, 1dc in each ch to end. *(24 sts)*
Row 2: 1ch, miss 1 st, *1htr in next st, 1tr in foll st, 3dtr in next st, 1tr in foll st, 1htr in next st, 1dc in foll st; rep from * ending last 1dc in 1-ch.
Row 3: Join B, miss first st, 1dc in each of next 3 sts, 3dc in next st (centre of 3-dtr), 1dc in each of next 2 sts, *dc3tog, 1dc in each of next 2 sts, 3dc in next st, 1dc in each of next 2 sts; rep from * to last st, dc2tog over last htr and 1-ch from previous row.
Row 4: Join C, miss first st, 1dc in each of next 3 sts, *3dc in next st (centre of 3-dc), 1dc in each of next 2 sts, dc3tog, 1dc in each of next 2 sts; rep from * to last 2 sts, dc2tog.
Row 5: Join A, 3ch, miss first st, 1dtr in next st, 1tr in foll st, *1htr in next st, 1dc in foll st, 1htr in next st, 1tr in foll st, dtr3tog, 1tr in next st; rep from * to last 2 sts, dtr2tog.
Row 6: Join C, miss 1 st, 1dc in each st to end, ending 1dc in last dtr. *(24 sts)*
Row 7: Join D, miss 1 st, 1dc in each st, ending 1dc in 1-ch. *(24 sts)*

Row 8: Join B, miss 1 st, 1dc in each st, ending 1dc in 1-ch. *(24 sts)*
Rep Rows 2–8 until work measures approx. 235cm (94in), ending on a Row 5.
Fasten off.

EDGING:

With RS facing, join A at beg of one long side, 1ch, work dc evenly along side, join with ss in corner st.
Fasten off.
Rep on other long side.

FINISHING

Sew in all ends.

CHAPTER 3
COLOURFUL
AND FUN HATS

Beanie Hat

A must-have basic beanie hat, crocheted in a supersoft wool and cashmere mix that looks and feels great.

SKILL RATING: ● ◉ ◉

YARN AND MATERIALS

Debbie Bliss Baby Cashmerino (55% wool/33% acrylic/12% cashmere, approx. 125m/137yd per 50g/1¾oz ball) 4ply (sport) weight yarn
  2 balls of shade 310 Lagoon (blue)

3.5mm (US size E/4) crochet hook

Yarn sewing needle

SIZE

One size

FINISHED MEASUREMENTS

50cm (19¾in) around, 18cm (7in) from crown to edge

TENSION

18 sts x 14 rows over a 10cm (4in) square working half treble, using a 3.5mm (US size E/4) hook and Debbie Bliss Baby Cashmerino.

ABBREVIATIONS

approx.	approximately
ch	chain
cont	continu(e)(ing)
dc	double crochet
htr	half treble
rep	repeat
RS	right side
ss	slip stitch
st(s)	stitch(es)
WS	wrong side
yrh	yarn round hook

SPECIAL ABBREVIATION

htr2tog (half treble 2 stitches together): [yrh, insert hook in next st, yrh, pull yarn through] twice (5 loops on hook), yrh, pull through all 5 loops on hook

HAT

Make 90ch, join with a ss in first ch to form a ring.
Round 1: 1ch, miss st at base of ch, 1dc in each ch, join with a ss in first ch. *(90 sts)*
Round 2: 1ch, miss st at base of ch, 1dc in each st, join with a ss in first ch.
Rounds 3–12: Rep Round 2.
Round 13: 2ch, miss st at base of ch, 1htr in each st to end, join with a ss in top of first 2-ch.
Rounds 14–24: Rep Round 13.
Round 25: 2ch, miss st at base of ch, *1htr in each of next 9 sts, htr2tog; rep from * to last st, 1htr in last st, join with a ss in top of first 2-ch. *(82 sts)*
Round 26: Rep Round 13.
Round 27: 2ch, miss st at base of ch, 1htr in each of next 8 sts, htr2tog; rep from * to last st, 1htr in last st, join with a ss in top of first 2-ch. *(74 sts)*
Round 28: Rep Round 13.
Round 29: 2ch, miss st at base of ch, *1htr in each of next 7 sts, htr2tog; rep from * to last st, 1htr in last st, join with a ss in top of first 2-ch. *(66 sts)*
Round 30: 2ch, miss st at base of ch, *1htr in each of next 6 sts, htr2tog; rep from * to last st, 1htr in last st, join with a ss in top of first 2-ch. *(58 sts)*
Round 31: 2ch, miss st at base of ch, *1htr in each of next 5 sts, htr2tog; rep from * to last st, 1htr in last st, join with a ss in top of first 2-ch. *(50 sts)*
Round 32: 2ch, miss st at base of ch, *1htr in each of next 4 sts, htr2tog; rep from * to last st, 1htr in last st, join with a ss in top of first 2-ch. *(42 sts)*
Round 33: 2ch, miss st at base of ch, *1htr in each of next 3 sts, htr2tog; rep from * to last st, 1htr in last st, join with a ss in top of first 2-ch. *(34 sts)*
Fasten off, leaving an approx. 20cm (8in) tail.

FINISHING

Working on WS of hat and using yarn needle, thread tail and insert needle through top of each st at top of hat, pull tightly to close hole and fasten off. Allow brim to roll up on RS.

Baby's Flower Bonnet

This little bonnet has a really vintage look with different pinks, purples and yellow flowers sewn onto a basic bonnet shape and tied with a pretty ribbon under the chin. It's a lovely warm, cosy hat for those chilly days walking in the park.

SKILL RATING: ● ● ◉

YARN AND MATERIALS

Debbie Bliss Baby Cashmerino
(55% wool/33% acrylic/12% cashmere, approx. 125m/137yd per 50g/1¾oz ball) 4ply (sport) weight yarn
    1 ball of shade 101 Ecru (off-white) (A)
    Scraps of each of shades:
    001 Primrose (yellow)
    101 Ecru (off-white)
    601 Baby Pink (light pink)
    006 Candy Pink (medium pink)
    700 Ruby (maroon)
    010 Lilac (purple)
    018 Citrus (green)
    608 Pale Lilac (lilac)

3mm (US size D/3) crochet hook

Yarn sewing needle

1m (40in) of 1.5cm (⅝in) wide ribbon

SIZE

To fit age 0–6 months

FINISHED MEASUREMENT

Approx. 37.5cm (15in) around

TENSION

15 sts x 8 rows over a 10cm (4in) square working treble, using a 3mm (US size D/3) hook and Debbie Bliss Baby Cashmerino.

ABBREVIATIONS

approx.	approximately
ch	chain
cont	continue
dc	double crochet
dtr	double treble
htr	half treble
rep	repeat
sp	space
ss	slip stitch
st(s)	stitch(es)
tr	treble
ttr	triple treble

BONNET

Using A, make 4ch, ss in first ch to form a ring.
Round 1: 2ch (counts as 1htr), 15htr in ring, join with a ss in top of first 2-ch. *(16 sts)*
Round 2: 3ch, 1tr in next st, 2tr in next and each st to end, join with a ss in top of first 3-ch. *(32 sts)*
Round 3: 3ch, 1tr in base of first 3-ch, *1tr in each of next 2 sts, 2tr in next st; rep from * around, join with a ss in top of first 3-ch. *(42 sts)*
Round 4: 3ch, 1tr in base of first 3-ch, *1tr in each of next 3 sts, 2tr in next st; rep from * around, join with a ss in top of first 3-ch. *(52 sts)*
Round 5: 3ch, 1tr in base of first 3-ch, 1tr in each st around, join with a ss in top of first 3-ch. *(52 sts)*
Round 6: 1ch, 1dc in between each tr to end, join with a ss in top of first 1-ch. *(52 sts)*
Rep Rounds 5 and 6 three times more.
Round 13: Rep Round 5.
Round 14: 1ch, *miss 1 st, 1dc in next st, miss 1 st, 5tr in next st (1 shell); rep from * until 8 shells are made ending 1dc, 1ss in next st.
Fasten off.

LAZY DAISY

(make approx. 7)
Using first colour, make 6ch, ss in first ch to form a ring.
Round 1: 1ch, 11dc in ring, join in next colour, ss to join in first 1-ch. *(12 sts)*

PETALS:
Cont with second colour.
Round 2: [9ch, ss in next st] 12 times, ending with a ss in ss of first round.
Weave around centre to close centre hole.
Fasten off.

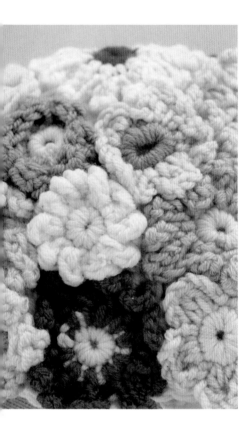

TIPS

Make enough flowers to fit all around the hat and completely cover the surface of the base bonnet.

Always sew in ends and weave in and out of stitches at the back of the flower centres to close the holes.

APPLE BLOSSOM

(make approx. 4)
Using first colour, make 4ch, ss in first ch to form a ring.
Round 1: 2ch, 9dc in ring, using second colour, ss in top of first 2-ch.
Cont with second colour.
Round 2: 1ch *[1dtr, 2ttr, 1dtr] in next st, ss in next st; rep from * 3 times more. [1dtr, 2ttr, 1dtr] in next st, ss in first 1-ch. *(5 petals)*
Fasten off.

PETAL BLOSSOM

(make approx. 10)
Using any colour, make 6ch, ss in first ch to form a ring.
16dc in ring, join with ss, *3ch, 1tr in each of next 2 sts, 3ch, ss in next st; rep from * 4 more times. *(5 petals)*
Weave around centre to close centre hole.
Fasten off.

REMEMBER ME BLOSSOM

(make approx. 5)
Using first colour, make 4ch, ss in first ch to form a ring.
Round 1: 2ch, 9dc in ring, using second colour, ss in top of first 2-ch. *(10 sts)*
Cont with second colour.
Round 2: 5ch, 1ttr in each of next 9 sts, ss in top of first 5-ch.
Fasten off.
Turn petals inside out.

CHERRY BLOSSOM

(make approx. 5)
Using any colour, make 4ch, ss in first ch to form a ring.
*3ch, 1tr in ring, 3ch, ss in ring; rep from * until 5 petals are made.
Fasten off.

FINISHING

Use a yarn sewing needle to weave the loose ends around the centre of the flowers to close the centre hole. Stitch the flowers to the bonnet. Sew in all ends.

Cut the ribbon in half and attach one end of each piece approx. 1cm (½in) down from last shell edge on each side.

Neil the Tiger

Cheeky and extremely cute, this is a great hat for wearing whilst practising tiger roars.

SKILL RATING: ● ● ○

YARN AND MATERIALS

Debbie Bliss Rialto DK (100% merino wool, approx. 105m/115yd per 50g/1¾oz ball) DK (light worsted) weight yarn
    1 ball each of shades:
    003 Black (A)
    043 Burnt Orange (dark orange) (B)
    002 Ecru (off-white) (C)

3.5mm (US size E/4) crochet hook

Yarn sewing needle

SIZE

To fit age 6–24 months

FINISHED MEASUREMENTS

Approx. 40.5–46cm (16–18in) around, 16.5cm (6½in) from crown to edge

TENSION

16 sts x 13 rows over a 10cm (4in) square working half treble, using a 3.5mm (US size E/4) hook and Debbie Bliss Rialto DK.

ABBREVIATIONS

approx.	approximately
beg	begin(ning)
ch	chain
cont	continu(e)(ing)
dc	double crochet
htr	half treble
rep	repeat
RS	right side
sp	space
ss	slip stitch
st(s)	stitch(es)

SPECIAL ABBREVIATION

htr2tog (half treble 2 stitches together): [yrh, insert hook in next st, yrh, pull yarn through] twice (5 loops on hook), yrh, pull through all 5 loops on hook

HAT

LOWER SECTION:

Work in rounds.

Using C, make 73ch, join with a ss in first ch. Insert st marker.

Round 1 (RS): 1ch (does not count as st), 1dc in next and each following ch to end. *(72 sts)*

Cut yarn and change to B in top of last st, so you are ready to start next round using B. Insert st marker.

Now beg working in spirals.

Round 2: Using B, 1htr in each st to end. *(72 sts)*

Round 3: Using B, 1htr in each st to end. *(72 sts)*

Round 4: Using A, 1htr in each st to end. *(72 sts)*

Cont to use colour sequence from Rounds 2–4 (two rounds B, one round A) throughout pattern.

Rounds 5–10: 1htr in each st to end. *(72 sts)*

MIDDLE SECTION:

Round 11: 1htr in each of next 23 sts, insert st marker, 1htr in each of next 23 sts, insert st marker (these two st markers mark beg and end of open part of face), 1htr in each of next 49 sts. Turn.

Work on these 49 sts only in rows (not rounds), changing colour at back of work and using colour sequence of two rows B, one row A as before.

Row 12: 2ch (does not count as st), 1htr in each of next 49 sts. Turn. *(49 sts)*

Row 13: 2ch (does not count as st), 1htr in each of next 49 sts. Do not turn.

Cont in rounds.

Round 14: Make 23ch, miss next 23 sts (from Round 8), miss first 2-ch (from start of Row 10), 1htr in each of next 25 sts (ending at centre back of hat).

Insert st marker to mark start of next round.

Round 15: 1htr in each of next 24 sts, 1htr in each of next 23 ch, 1htr in each of next 25 sts. *(72 sts – it's very important to have correct number of sts at end of this round)*

Round 16: Use A on this round. Do not change colour when you get to B sts used on front 23 ch, cont using A. 1htr in each st to end. *(72 sts)*

Round 17: 1htr in each st to end. *(72 sts)*

TIPS

This hat is worked from the bottom to the top. It has a mix of rounds and rows, so check carefully when rounds turn into rows and rows turn into rounds, and use stitch markers to mark the beginning of each round.

The stripe is made up of 2 rows of orange and 1 row black.

When changing colour, cut the yarn and join the new yarn in the top of the last stitch (see page 108), so you are ready to start the next round using the new colour.

Keep colour changes on top of each other as you go up in rounds, so that joins remain in line from top to bottom of the hat and at the back.

TOP SECTION:

Beg decreases.

Cont following rounds, changing colour at join in line from bottom to top of hat.

Round 18: *1htr in each of next 10 sts, htr2tog; rep from * to end. *(66 sts)*

Round 19: *1htr in each of next 9 sts, htr2tog; rep from * to end. *(60 sts)*

Round 20: *1htr in each of next 8 sts, htr2tog; rep from * to end. *(54 sts)*

Round 21: *1htr in each of next 7 sts, htr2tog; rep from * to end. *(48 sts)*

Round 22: *1htr in each of next 6 sts, htr2tog; rep from * to end. *(42 sts)*

Round 23: *1htr in each of next 5 sts, htr2tog; rep from * to end. *(36 sts)*

Round 24: *1htr in each of next 4 sts, htr2tog; rep from * to end. *(30 sts)*

Round 25: *1htr in each of next 3 sts, htr2tog; rep from * to end. *(24 sts)*

Round 26: *1htr in each of next 2 sts, htr2tog; rep from * to end. *(18 sts)*

Round 27: *1htr in next st, htr2tog; rep from * to end. *(12 sts)*

Round 28: Htr2tog around. *(6 sts)*

Fasten off.

FACE EDGING:

With RS facing, join C in first st of bottom face edge.

1ch, 1dc in same st, 1dc in each of next 22 sts, 7dc evenly along side of face edge, 21dc evenly along top of face edge, 7dc evenly along other side of face edge, join with a ss in first dc.

EARS

(make 2)

Work in rounds, placing st marker at beg of each round. Using C, make 2ch.

Round 1: 6dc in second ch from hook.

Round 2: 2dc in each st to end. *(12 sts)*

Round 3: *1dc in each of next 2 sts, 2dc in next st; rep from * to end. *(16 sts)*

Cut off C, join B.

Round 4: Cont with B, *1dc in each of next 3 sts, 2dc in next st; rep from * to end. *(20 sts)*

Rounds 5–8: 1dc in each st to end. *(20 sts)*

Ss in next st.

Fasten off, leaving a long tail for sewing on.

FINISHING

Sew in all ends.

Pin each ear onto the hat, starting approx. 3 rows down from the top centre of the hat. Sew the ears in place.

Baby's Sailboat Hat

A really simple beanie hat pattern decorated with a pretty boat motif. Always use a very soft yarn if making something that will be worn on a baby's head.

SKILL RATING: ● ● ●

YARN AND MATERIALS

Debbie Bliss Baby Cashmerino (55% wool/33% acrylic/12% cashmere, approx. 125m/137yd per 50g/1¾oz ball) 4ply (sport) weight yarn
1 ball each of shades:
101 Ecru (off-white) (A)
072 Kingfisher (turquoise) (B)
026 Duck Egg (pale blue) (C)
Scraps of red, white and blue

3mm (US size D/3) and 2.5mm (US size C/2) crochet hooks

Yarn sewing needle

SIZE

To fit age 3–6 months

FINISHED MEASUREMENT

36cm (14in) around

TENSION

18 sts x 13 rows over a 10cm (4in) square working half treble, using a 3mm (US size D/3) hook and Debbie Bliss Baby Cashmerino.

ABBREVIATIONS

approx.	approximately
ch	chain
cont	continue
dc	double crochet
dtr	double treble
htr	half treble
rep	repeat
ss	slip stitch
st(s)	stitch(es)
tr	treble
ttr	triple treble
qtr	quadruple treble
WS	wrong side

HAT

Using A and 3mm (US size D/3) hook, make 4ch, ss in first ch to make a ring.
Round 1: 2ch, make 8htr into ring, join with a ss in first 2-ch. *(8 sts)*
Round 2: 2ch, 1htr in same st, 2htr in each st to end, join with a ss in first 2-ch. *(16 sts)*
Round 3: 2ch, 1htr in same st, *1htr in next st, 2htr in next st; rep from * to end, join with a ss in first 2-ch. *(24 sts)*
Round 4: Rep Round 3. *(36 sts)*
Round 5: 2ch, 1htr in same st, *1htr in each of next 2 sts, 2htr in next st; rep from * to last 2 sts, 1htr in each of last 2 sts, join with a ss in first 2-ch. *(48 sts)*
Round 6: 2ch, 1htr in same st, *1htr in each of next 7 sts, 2htr in next st; rep from * to last 7 sts, 1htr in each st to end, join with a ss in first 2-ch. *(54 sts)*
Round 7: 2ch, 1htr in same st, *1htr in each of next 8 sts, 2htr in next st; rep from * to last 8 sts, 1htr in each st to end, join with a ss in first 2-ch. *(60 sts)*
Rounds 8–14: 2ch, 1htr in each st to end, join with a ss in first 2-ch.
Join in B.
Round 15: 1ch, 1dc in each st to end, join with a ss.
Join in C.
Round 16: 1ch, 1dc in each st to end, join with a ss.
Fasten off.

BOAT MOTIF BASE

Using red and 2.5mm (US size C/2) hook, make 9ch, 1dc in next ch from hook, 1htr in next ch, 1tr in next ch, 1dtr in next ch, 1tr in next ch, 1htr in next ch, 1dc, ss in first ch.
Fasten off.

BOAT MOTIF SAILS

Using white and 2.5mm (US size C/2) hook, make 11ch, 1dc in second ch from hook, 1dc in next ch, 1htr in next ch, 1tr in each of next 2 ch, 1dtr in next ch, 1ttr in next ch, 1qtr in next ch.
Fasten off.
Working on other side of ch just worked with WS facing, join blue in underside of second dc, 1dc in next ch, 1htr in next ch, 1tr in next ch, 1dtr in next ch, 1ttr in next ch, 1qtr in next ch, 6ch, join with a ss in next ch.
Fasten off, leaving a long tail for sewing on.

FINISHING

Sew in all ends on the hat.

Sew the boat motif sails onto the boat motif base using the yarn tail threaded into the yarn sewing needle, attaching it to the centre bottom chain of the straighter edge of the bottom edge of the boat.

Sew the boat motif onto the hat.

CHAPTER 4
CREATIVE SCARVES, COWLS AND CAPES

Chevron and Daisy Scarf

This is a really lovely stitch to use and the wave stitch is fast to work. The design makes a great scarf for men or women; for a man just omit the flowers!

SKILL RATING: ● ● ◐

YARN AND MATERIALS

Debbie Bliss Cashmerino Aran (55% merino wool/33% acrylic/ 12% cashmere, approx. 90m/98yd per 50g/1¾oz ball) Aran (worsted) weight yarn

6 balls of shade 064 Cowslip (yellow) (A)
1 ball of shade 101 Ecru (off-white) (B)

Debbie Bliss Rialto DK (100% merino wool, approx. 105m/115yd per 50g/1¾oz ball) DK (light worsted) weight yarn

1 ball each of shades:
057 Banana (yellow) (C)
101 Ecru (off-white) (D)

3mm (US size D/3) and 4.5mm (US size 7) crochet hooks

Yarn sewing needle

Sewing needle and off-white thread

MEASUREMENTS

Approx. 18.5 x 228cm (7¼ x 91¼in)

TENSION

14 sts x 11 rows over a 10cm (4in) square working wave and chevron stitch pattern, using a 4.5mm (US size 7) hook and Debbie Bliss Cashmerino Aran.

ABBREVIATIONS

approx. approximately
ch chain
cont continu(e)(ing)
dc double crochet
dc2tog double crochet 2 stitches together
dtr double treble
htr half treble
patt pattern
rep repeat
RS right side
ss slip stitch
st(s) stitch(es)
tr treble
yrh yarn round hook

SPECIAL ABBREVIATIONS

dc3tog (double crochet 3 stitches together): [insert hook in next st, yrh, pull yarn through] 3 times, yrh, pull through all 4 loops on hook

dtr2tog (double treble 2 stitches together): *yrh twice, insert hook in next st, yrh, pull yarn through, [yrh, pull through first 2 loops on hook] twice; rep from * once more, yrh, pull through all 3 loops on hook

dtr3tog (double treble 3 stitches together): *yrh twice, insert hook in next st, yrh, pull yarn through, [yrh, pull through first 2 loops on hook] twice; rep from * twice more, yrh, pull through all 4 loops on hook

SCARF

Using A and 4.5mm (US size 7) hook, make 26ch.

Row 1 (RS): 1dc in 2nd ch from hook, 1dc in each ch to end. *(25 sts)*
Row 2: 1ch, 1dc in first dc, *1htr in next dc, 1tr in next dc, 3dtr in next dc, 1tr in next dc, 1htr in next dc, 1dc in next dc; rep from * to end.
Row 3: 1ch, dc2tog over first 2 sts (dc and htr), 1dc in each of next 2 sts, 3dc in next st (centre dtr of 3-dtr group), 1dc in each of next 2 sts, *dc3tog over next 3 sts, 1dc in each of next 2 sts, 3dc in next st, 1dc in each of next 2 sts; rep from * to last 2 sts, dc2tog over last 2 sts (htr and dc).
Row 4: 1ch, dc2tog over first 2 dc (dc and htr), 1dc in each of next 2 dc, 3dc in next dc (centre dc of 3-dc group), 1dc in each of next 2 dc, *dc3tog over next 3 dc, 1dc in each of next 2 dc, 3dc in next dc, 1dc in each of next 2 dc; rep from * to last 2 sts, dc2tog over last 2 dc.
Row 5: 4ch, miss first st, 1dtr in next st, 1tr in next st, 1htr in next st, 1dc in next st (centre dc of 3-dc group), 1htr in next st, 1tr in next st, *dtr3tog over next 3 sts, 1tr in next st, 1htr in next st, 1dc in next st, 1htr in next st, 1tr in next st; rep from * to last 2 sts, dtr2tog over last 2 sts.
Row 6: 1ch, 1dc in each st to end, working last dc in last dtr. *(25 sts)*
Row 7: 1ch, 1dc in each dc to end.
Rows 8–13: Rep Rows 2–7 once.
Rows 14–17: Rep Rows 2–5 once.
Cut off A, but do not fasten off.
Rows 18–19: Join B and rep Rows 6 and 7.
Cut off B, but do not fasten off.
Row 20: Join A and rep Row 2.
[Rep Rows 3–20] 12 times more, then Rows 3–19 once – work measures approx. 228cm (91¼in).
Do not fasten off, but cont with A to work edging.

EDGING:
With RS facing and using A and 4.5mm (US size 7) hook, work 2dc in corner, then work dc evenly along row-end edge, 2dc in corner, 1dc in each foundation ch, 2dc in corner, work dc evenly along remaining row-end edge, 2 dc in corner, join with a ss in first dc of last row of scarf. Fasten off.

FLOWERS

(make 13)
Using C and 3mm (US size D/3) hook, make 4ch, join with a ss in first ch to form a ring.

Round 1 (RS): 1ch, 11dc in ring, cut off C, join D with a ss in first dc. Cont with RS facing.
Round 2: 11ch, 1ss in same dc as last ss, [11ch, 1ss in next dc] 11 times, join with a ss at base of first 11ch. *(12 petals)*
Fasten off.

FINISHING

Sew in ends. On flowers, weave yarn end around centre hole to close.

The WS and RS are not hugely different on this scarf, so sew the flowers on either side in the centre of each off-white line, using sewing thread around the tips of each petal and in the centre to secure.

Lace Scarf

I'm a big fan of light scarves and this scarf is beautifully delicate and pretty. The yarn is a mix of silk and merino and the stitch light and textured.

YARN AND MATERIALS

Fyberspates Scrumptious Lace (55% merino wool/45% silk, approx. 1000m/1094yd per 100g/3½oz hank) laceweight yarn
   1 hank of shade 507 Teal (blue)

5mm (US size H/8) crochet hook

Yarn sewing needle

FINISHED MEASUREMENTS

26.5 x 133cm (10½ x 52½in)

TENSION

18 sts x 10 rows over a 10cm (4in) square working treble, using a 5mm (US size H/8) hook and Fyberspates Scrumptious Lace.

3 fans x 10 rows over a 10cm (4in) square working Fan and V-st pattern, using a 5mm (US size H/8) hook and Fyberspates Scrumptious Lace.

ABBREVIATIONS

approx.	approximately
beg	begin(ning)
ch	chain
cont	continue
dc	double crochet
htr	half treble
rep	repeat
RS	right side
sp(s)	space(s)
ss	slip stitch
st(s)	stitch(es)
tr	treble
yrh	yarn round hook

SPECIAL ABBREVIATIONS

Fan: work [3tr, 1ch, 3tr] all in same place

V-st (V-stitch): work [1htr, 1ch, 1htr] all in same place

2trCL (2-treble cluster): [yrh, insert hook in sp, yrh, pull yarn through work, yrh, pull yarn through first 2 loops on hook] twice in same sp (3 loops on hook), yrh and pull yarn through all 3 loops on hook

3-ch picot (3-chain picot): make 3ch, ss in third ch from hook

SCARF

Make 82ch.

Row 1 (RS): 1dc in 2nd ch from hook, 1dc in next ch, *miss 3 ch, Fan in next ch, miss 3 ch, 1dc in next ch**, 1ch, miss 1 ch, 1dc in next ch; rep from * ending last rep at **, 1dc in last ch.

Row 2: 2ch (counts as first htr), 1htr in first dc, *2ch, 1dc in 1-ch sp at centre of next Fan, 2ch**, V-st in 1-ch sp between next 2 dc; rep from * ending last rep at **, miss next dc, 2htr in last dc.

Row 3: 3ch (counts as first tr), 3tr in first htr, *1dc in next 2-ch sp, 1ch, 1dc in next 2-ch sp**, Fan in 1-ch sp at centre of next V-st; rep from * ending last rep at **, 4tr in top of 2-ch at end of row.

Row 4: 1ch, 1dc in first tr, *2ch, V-st in next 1-ch sp between next 2 dc, 2ch**, 1dc in 1-ch sp at centre of next Fan; rep from * ending last rep at **, 1dc in top of 3-ch at end of row.

Row 5: 1ch, 1dc in first dc, *1dc in next 2-ch sp, Fan in 1-ch sp at centre of next V-st, 1dc in next 2-ch sp **, 1ch; rep from * ending last rep at **, 1dc in last dc.

Rep Rows 2–5 until scarf measures 123cm (48½in), ending on a Row 2 (a WS row).

Do not fasten off, but work top edging along this last row.

TOP EDGING:

With RS facing, beg picot-shell edging across last row of scarf as follows:

Row 1 (RS): 4ch (counts as first tr and 1-ch sp), 1tr in first htr, *[2trCL, 3ch, 2trCL] in next dc (at centre of Fan)**, [1tr, 3ch, 1tr] in 1-ch sp at centre of next V-st; rep from * ending last rep at **, [1tr, 1ch, 1tr] in 2-ch at end of row.

Row 2: 4ch, 1tr in first tr, *[2trCL, 3ch, 2trCL] in 3-ch sp at centre of next 2 clusters**, [1tr, 3ch, 1tr] in next 3-ch sp at centre of next '1tr, 3ch, 1tr' group; rep from * ending last rep at **, [1tr, 1ch, 1tr] in 4-ch sp at end of row.

Row 3: 1ch, 1dc in first tr, 2ch, *5tr in next 3-ch sp (between clusters), 2ch**, 1dc in next 3-ch sp (between trebles), 2ch; rep from * ending last rep at **, 1dc in 4-ch sp at end of row.

Row 4 (picot row): 1ss in first dc, *1ch, [1dc in next tr, 3-ch picot] 5 times, 1ss in same place as last dc was worked, 1ch, 1ss in next dc; rep from * to end of row.

Fasten off.

BOTTOM EDGING:

Work other edging along underside of foundation chain at other end of scarf. With RS facing, join with a ss in first ch of foundation chain and work picot-shell edging as follows:

Row 1 (RS): 4ch (counts as first tr and 1-ch sp), 1tr in same foundation ch, *[2trCL, 3ch, 2trCL] in centre of bottom of next Fan**, [1tr, 3ch, 1tr] in next 1-ch sp (between 2 dc in Row 1 of scarf); rep from * ending last rep at **, [1tr, 1ch, 1tr] in last foundation ch.

Rows 2–4: Work as for Rows 2–4 of top edging.

Fasten off.

FINISHING

Sew in the yarn ends. Do not press.

Floral Lace Scarf

This is a very easy stitch to achieve, but the scarf is rated at a higher level because of the very fine alpaca yarn used – if you make a mistake, it is very difficult to undo. Practise the stitch using some scraps of double knitting or Aran-weight yarn to master the techniques before you start.

SKILL RATING: ● ● ●

YARN AND MATERIALS

Rowan Fine Lace (80% baby alpaca/20% merino wool, approx. 400m/437yd per 50g/1¾oz ball) laceweight yarn

2 balls of shade 944 White (A)
1 ball each of shades:
953 Ruby (deep pink) (B)
920 Cameo (beige) (C)

3mm (US size D/3) and 3.5mm (US size E/4) crochet hooks

Yarn sewing needle

FINISHED MEASUREMENTS

Approx. 63 x 145cm (25 x 57in)

TENSION

7 ch sps x 6 rows over a 10cm (4in) square working scarf pattern, using a 3.5mm (US size E/4) hook and Rowan Fine Lace.

ABBREVIATIONS

approx.	approximately
beg	beginning
ch	chain
ch sp	chain space
cont	continue
dc	double crochet
patt	pattern
rep	repeat
RS	right side
sp(s)	space(s)
ss	slip stitch
st(s)	stitch(es)
tr	treble

SCARF

Using A and 3.5mm (US size E/4) hook, make 178ch.
Row 1: 1dc in 6th ch from hook *5ch, miss 3 ch, 1dc in next ch; rep from * to end. *(44 sps)*
Row 2: *5ch, 1dc in next 5-ch sp; rep from * to end.
Rep Row 2 until work measures approx. 145cm (57in) – smooth out the scarf in both directions to measure length.
Do not fasten off, but work edging as follows.

EDGING:
Round 1 (RS): Working along first long row-end edge, make 1ch, 1dc in top of next ch (first corner), 3dc in each sp to next corner; working along short foundation-chain edge, 1dc in top of corner ch (second corner), 3dc in each sp to next corner; working along second long row-end edge, work 1dc in top of corner ch (third corner), 3dc in each sp to next corner; working along short top edge (along last row of scarf), work 1dc in top of corner ch (fourth corner), 3dc in each sp to end, join with a ss in first dc.
Fasten off.
Round 2 (loop round): With RS facing, join A with a ss in corner st at beg of one short edge (foundation-chain edge or 'last-row' edge), then working along first short edge, make 1ch, 1dc in same st, [16ch, 1dc in next st, 1dc in each of next 6 sts, 4ch, 1dc in same place as last dc, *1dc in each of next 5 sts, 16ch, 1dc in same place as last dc, 1dc in each of next 5 sts, 4ch, 1dc in same place as last dc, rep from * to corner, 1dc in each dc to corner, 1dc in corner, 16ch, 1dc in next st – 27 loops made]; working along first long edge, ***measure this edge and place pin markers equally spaced apart in 31 places (for loops), then work 1dc in each st to pin marker, **at pin marker work 4ch, 1dc in same place as last dc, 1dc in each st to next pin marker, rep from ** to next corner***; working along second short edge, work 1dc in corner, rep section between square brackets; working along second long edge, rep from *** to ***, join with a ss in first dc.
Fasten off.

LARGE FLOWERS

(make 29 two-colour flowers and 25 one-colour flowers)
Using B or C and 3mm (US size D/3) hook, make 6ch, join with a ss in first ch to form a ring.
Round 1 (RS): 15dc in ring, enclosing yarn tail inside all dc around circle, cut off yarn, join in B or C with a ss in first dc.
Cont with RS facing.
Round 2: *3ch, 1tr in each of next 2 sts, 3ch, 1ss in next st; rep from * 4 times more, working last ss in first dc. *(5 petals)*
Fasten off.
Pull tail to close up centre hole or sew hole to close with a yarn needle.

SMALL FLOWERS

(make 62)
Using B and 3mm (US size D/3) hook, make 4ch, join with a ss in first ch to form a ring.
Round 1: [3ch, 1ss in ring] 5 times, join with a ss in base of first 3ch.
Fasten off.
Sew around hole in centre to close.

FINISHING

Sew in all ends.

Sew a large flower onto the tip of each loop made on Round 2 of the edging along the short ends of the scarf.

Using C, embroider one French knot (see page 111) in the centre of each small flower. Sew the small flowers onto the loops made on Round 2 of the edging along the long edges of the scarf.

When all the flowers are stitched on, sew adjacent petals of the large flowers to each other.

Wave and Chevron Stitch Scarf

YARN AND MATERIALS

Debbie Bliss Cashmerino Aran (55% merino wool/33% microfibre/12% cashmere, approx. 90m/98yd per 50g/1¾oz ball) Aran (worsted) weight yarn
2 balls each of shades:
    042 Mulberry (purple) (A)
    027 Stone (pale grey) (B)
    082 Duck Egg (blue-green) (C)
    603 Baby Pink (pale pink) (D)

5mm (US size H/8) crochet hook

Yarn sewing needle

FINISHED MEASUREMENTS

Approx. 19 x 228.5cm (7½ x 90in)

TENSION

15 sts x 9 rows over a 10cm (4in) square working treble crochet, using a 5mm (US size H/8) hook and Debbie Bliss Cashmerino Aran.

ABBREVIATIONS

approx. approximately
ch chain
rep repeat
st(s) stitch(es)
tr treble
yrh yarn round hook

SPECIAL ABBREVIATION

tr3tog (treble crochet 3 stitches together): *yrh, insert hook in next st, yrh, pull yarn through, yrh, pull yarn through first 2 loops on hook; rep from * in each of next 2 sts (4 loops on hook), yrh, pull yarn through all 4 loops on hook

Note: Work the scarf in a repeating stripe sequence of 1 row A, 1 row B, 1 row C and 1 row D.

Stripes are great on scarves or blankets and combining them with wave and chevron stitch makes a very effective and interesting project. The stitch is one of my favourites – once you get the idea of the increases and decreases it's a very therapeutic stitch to use, and it's fun to experiment with the stripes. Don't be deterred by all the sewing in of ends – that can be therapeutic too!

SCARF

Using A, make 33ch.
Row 1: 1tr in 3rd ch from hook, 1tr in each of next 3 ch, tr3tog over next 3 ch, 1tr in each of next 3 ch, *3tr in next ch, 1tr in each of next 3 ch, tr3tog over next 3 ch, 1tr in each of next 3 ch; rep from * to last ch, 2tr in last ch. Cut off yarn, but do not fasten off.
Row 2: Join next colour, 3ch, 1tr in each of first 4 sts, tr3tog over next 3 sts, 1tr in each of next 3 sts, *3tr in next st, 1tr in each of next 3 sts, tr3tog over next 3 sts, 1tr in each of next 3 sts; rep from * to end, 2tr in top of 3-ch at end of row.
Rep Row 2, changing colour on each row, until work measures approx. 228.5cm (90in) from beginning or until you run out of yarn, ending with A.
Fasten off.

FINISHING

Sew in all yarn ends.

Swishy Scarf

This scarf is made with half trebles in the middle and is crocheted horizontally, with a lacy edging. If you are a beginner, make 4–5 more rows of half trebles than in the pattern; if you are an intermediate crochet worker, have a go at the pretty edging.

SKILL RATING: ● ● ○

YARN AND MATERIALS

Debbie Bliss Rialto DK (100% merino wool, approx. 105m/115yd per 50g/1¾oz ball) DK (light worsted) weight yarn
   3 balls of shade 002 Ecru (off-white)

4mm (US size F/5) crochet hook

Yarn sewing needle

FINISHED MEASUREMENTS

Approx. 157 x 11cm (62 x 4½in)

TENSION

Tension is not critical on this project.

ABBREVIATIONS

approx.	approximately
ch	chain
ch sp	chain space
dc	double crochet
dtr	double treble
htr	half treble
rep	repeat
ss	slip stitch
st(s)	stitch(es)
tr	treble

SCARF

Make 258ch.
Row 1: 1htr in second ch from hook, 1htr in each ch to end.
Rows 2–3: 2ch, 1htr in each st to end. Do not fasten off.

EDGING:
Work in rounds, not in rows. Do not turn at end of round.
Round 1: *3ch, miss 3 sts, 1dc in next st**; rep from * to ** until first corner, 3ch, 1dc into middle of second row of side edge, 3ch, 1dc in next corner; rep from * to ** to next corner, 3ch, 1dc into middle of second row of side edge, 3ch, join with a ss in base of first 3-ch.
Round 2: 2tr, 3ch, 2tr in middle st of first 3-ch from previous round. *2tr, 3ch, 2tr into middle st of next 3-ch from previous round; rep from * to end of round, join with a ss in top of first 2-tr.
Round 3: Ss in middle st of first 3-ch from previous round, *5ch, ss in middle st of next 3-ch from previous round; rep from * to end, 5ch, ss in first ss.
Round 4: *5dc in 5-ch sp; rep from * to end, join with a ss in ss from previous round.
Round 5: *1dc in first st, 1ch, 1htr, 1ch, 1tr in next st, [1ch, 1dtr, 1ch] 3 times in next st, 1tr, 1ch, 1htr in next st, 1ch, 1dc in next st, ss in ss from previous round; rep from * to end, join with a ss in ss from previous round.
Fasten off.

FINISHING

Sew in all ends.

Chunky Seashell Scarf

Chunky scarves are really popular in all the high street fashion shops, so why not make your own? This project uses beautifully soft chunky wool, has a really contemporary designer look and only takes a couple of evenings to make. What could be better!

SKILL RATING: ● ● ○

YARN AND MATERIALS

Rowan Big Wool (100% merino wool, 80m/87yd per 100g/3½oz ball) super-chunky (super-bulky) weight yarn
    4 balls of shade 021 Ice Blue
    (pale blue)

7mm (US size K10½) crochet hook

Yarn sewing needle

FINISHED MEASUREMENTS

Approx. 25.5 x 148cm (10 x 58in)

TENSION

Tension is not critical on this project.

ABBREVIATIONS

approx. approximately
ch chain
ch sp chain space
dc double crochet
dtr double treble
rep repeat
sp space
ss slip stitch
st(s) stitch(es)
tch turning chain

SCARF

Make 20ch very loosely.

Row 1: Working very loosely on this row, 1dc in second ch from hook and in each following ch to end.

Row 2: 1dc in first st, *miss 4 sts, 7dtr in next st, 1dc in next st; rep from * to end.

Row 3: 4ch, 1dtr in first dc from previous row, *3ch, miss 3 sts, 1dc in top of next st (top of fan), 3ch, miss 3 sts, 2dtr in top of dc from last row (between shells); rep from *, ending row with 2dtr in last dc of previous row.

Row 4: 1ch, 1dc in next st, *miss next ch sp, 7dtr in top of dc from previous row, miss 3ch, 1dc in sp between 2 dtr from previous row; rep from *, ending row with 1dc in sp between last dtr and tch.

Rep Rows 3 and 4 until scarf measures approx. 146.5cm (57½in), ending with a Row 4.

Last row: 1ch, *1dc in each 7-dtr from previous row, 1ch, 1dc between shells, 1ch; rep from * to end, finishing with 1ch, ss in last st.

Fasten off.

FINISHING

Sew in all ends.

Red Petal Cape

SKILL RATING: ● ● ●

YARN AND MATERIALS

Debbie Bliss Baby Cashmerino (55% wool/33% acrylic/12% cashmere, approx. 125m/137yd per 50g/1¾oz ball) 4ply (sport) weight yarn
  3:**4**:5 balls of shade 700 Ruby (red) (A)

Debbie Bliss Rialto DK (100% merino wool, approx. 105m/115yd per 50g/1¾oz ball) DK (light worsted) weight yarn
  1 ball of shade 066 Vintage Pink (pale pink) (B)

3.5mm (US size E/4) crochet hook

Yarn sewing needle

SIZE

To fit age: 3–12:**18–24**:24–36 months

FINISHED MEASUREMENTS

Small: 76.5cm (30½in) around, 30cm (12in) long
Medium: 86.5cm (34¼in) around, 35cm (14in) long
Large: 95cm (38in) around, 37cm (14¾in) long

TENSION

3½ shell patterns x 8 rows over a 10cm (4in) square, using a 3.5mm (US size E/4) hook and Debbie Bliss Baby Cashmerino.

ABBREVIATIONS

approx.	approximately
ch	chain
ch sp	chain space
cont	continue
dc	double crochet
patt	pattern
rep	repeat
RS	right side
sp	space
ss	slip stitch
st(s)	stitch(es)
tr	treble
yrh	yarn round hook

A really sweet little cape made using an open shell stitch on the petals, and with a 'crocodile stitch' collar making scales or scallops around the neck.

MAIN BODY

Using A, make 91:**99**:107ch.
Row 1: 1tr in 3rd ch from hook, *1ch, miss 2 ch, [1tr, 3ch, 1tr] in next ch, 1ch, miss 2 ch, 1tr in each of next 3 ch; rep from * to end, omitting 1tr at end of last rep. *(89:**97**:105 sts)*
Row 2: 4ch (counts as 1tr, 1ch), 7tr in next 3-ch sp, *1ch, miss 2 tr, 1tr in next tr, 1ch, 7tr in next 3-ch sp; rep from * to last 3 tr, 1ch, miss 2 tr, 1tr in top of 3-ch.
Row 3: 4ch, 1tr in base of 4-ch, 1ch, miss 2 tr, 1tr in each of next 3 tr, *1ch, miss 2 tr, [1tr, 3ch, 1tr] in next tr, 1ch, miss 2 tr, 1tr in each of next 3 tr; rep from * to last 3 tr, miss 2 tr, [1tr, 1ch, 1tr] in third of 4-ch from previous row.
Row 4: 3ch (counts as 1tr), 3tr in first ch sp, 1ch, miss 2 tr, 1tr in next tr, *1ch, 7tr in next 3-ch sp, 1ch, miss 2 tr, 1tr in next tr; rep from * to last 3 tr, 1ch, miss 2 tr, 3tr in last ch sp, 1tr in third of 4-ch from previous row.
Row 5: 3ch, miss 1 tr, 1tr in next tr, *1ch, miss 2 tr, [1tr, 3ch, 1tr] in next tr, 1ch, miss 2 tr, 1tr in each of next 3 tr; rep from * to end, omitting one tr at end of last rep and placing last tr in third of 3-ch from previous row.
Row 6: 4ch (counts as 1tr, 1ch), 9tr in next 3-ch sp, *2ch, miss 3 tr, 1tr in next tr, 2ch, 9tr in next 3-ch sp; rep from * to last 3 tr, 2ch, miss 2 tr, 1tr in top of 3-ch.
Row 7: 4ch, 1tr in base of 4-ch, 2ch, miss 3 tr, 1tr in each of next 3 tr, *2ch, miss 2 tr [1tr, 3ch, 1tr] in next tr, 2ch, miss 3 tr, 1tr in each of next 3 tr; rep from * to last 3 tr, 2ch, miss 3 tr, [1tr, 1ch, 1tr] in third of 4-ch.
Row 8: 3ch (counts as 1tr), 3tr in first ch sp, 2ch, miss 2 tr, 1tr in next tr, *2ch, 9tr in next 3-ch sp, 2ch, miss 2 tr, 1tr in next tr; rep from * to last

3 tr, 2ch, miss 2 tr, 3tr in last ch sp, 1tr in third of 4-ch.
Row 9: 3ch, miss 1 tr, 1tr in next tr, 2ch, miss 2 tr, [1tr, 3ch, 1tr] in next tr, *2ch, miss 3 tr, 1tr in each of next 3 tr, 2ch, miss 3 tr, [1tr, 3ch, 1tr] in next tr; rep from * to last 3 tr, make 2ch, miss 1 tr, 1tr in each of next 2 tr, 1tr in third of 4-ch.
Row 10: Rep Row 6.
Row 11: 4ch, 1tr in base of 4-ch, 2ch, miss 3 tr, 1tr in next tr, 2tr in next tr, 1tr in next tr, *2ch, miss 3 tr, [1tr, 3ch, 1tr] in next tr, 2ch, miss 3 tr, 1tr in next tr, 2tr in next tr, 1tr in next tr; rep from * to last 3 tr, 2ch, miss 3 tr, [1tr, 1ch, 1tr] in third of 4-ch from previous row.
Row 12: 3ch, 3tr in first ch sp, 2ch, miss 2 tr, 1tr in each of next 2 tr, miss 1 tr, *2ch, 9tr in next 3-ch sp, 2ch, miss 1 tr, 1tr in each of next 2 tr, miss 1 tr; rep from * to last 2-ch sp, 2ch miss 2-ch sp, 3tr in last 4-ch sp, 1tr in top of 3-ch from previous row.
Row 13: 3ch, miss 1 tr, 1tr in next tr, 2ch, miss 2 tr, *1tr in next tr, 5ch, 1tr in next tr, 2ch**, miss 3 tr, 1tr in next tr, 2tr in next tr, 1tr in next tr, 2ch, miss 3 tr; rep from * to last rep, ending at **, miss 1 tr, 1tr in each of next 3 tr, 1tr in top of 3-ch from previous row.
Row 14: 5ch, 11tr in next 5-ch sp, *3ch, miss 1 tr, 1tr in each of next 2 tr, miss 1 tr, 3ch, 11tr in next 5-ch sp; rep from * to last tr, 2ch, miss 1 tr, 1tr in top of 3-ch from previous row.
Row 15: 5ch, 1tr in base of 5-ch, *3ch, miss 4 tr, 1tr in next tr, 2tr in next tr, 1tr in next tr, miss 4 tr, 3ch, 1tr in next tr, 5ch, 1tr in next tr; rep from * to last 11 tr from previous row, miss 4 tr, 3ch, 1tr in next tr, 2tr in next tr, 1tr in next tr, miss 4 tr, 3ch, 1tr in 3rd of 5-ch from previous row.

Row 3: 7ch, 1dc in next 3-ch sp, *3ch, 1dc in next ch sp; rep from * 5 times more, 4ch, 1tr in third ch of 7-ch from previous row.

Row 4: 7ch, 1dc in next 3-ch sp, *3ch, 1dc in next ch sp; rep from * 4 times more, 4ch, 1tr in third ch of 7-ch from previous row.

Row 5: 7ch, 1dc in next 3-ch sp, *3ch, 1dc in next ch sp; rep from * 3 times more, 4ch, 1tr in third ch of 7-ch from previous row.

Row 6: 7ch, 1dc in next 3-ch sp, *3ch, 1dc in next ch sp; rep from * twice more, 4ch, 1tr in third ch of 7-ch from previous row.

Row 7: 7ch, 1dc in next 3-ch sp, *3ch, 1dc in next ch sp; rep from * once more, 4ch, 1tr in third ch of 7-ch from previous row.

Row 8: 7ch, 1dc in next 3-ch sp, 4ch, 1tr in third ch of 7-ch from previous row.

Row 9: 7ch, 1tr in dc, 4ch, 1tr in third ch of 7-ch from previous row.

Row 10: 3ch, 1dtr in tr, 3ch, ss in third ch of 7-ch from previous row.
Fasten off.

SIZES **18–24**:24–36 MONTHS ONLY:

Row 16: 3ch, 4tr in first ch sp, 3ch, miss 1 tr, 1tr in each of next 2 tr, miss 1 tr, *3ch, 11tr in next 5-ch sp, 3ch, miss 1 tr, 1tr in each of next 2 tr, miss 1 tr; rep from * to last 3-ch sp, 3ch miss 3-ch sp, 4tr in last 5-ch sp.

Row 17: 3ch, miss 1 tr, 1tr in next tr, 3ch, miss 2 tr, *1tr in next tr, 5tr, 1tr in next tr, 3ch**, miss 4 tr, 1tr in next tr, 2tr in next tr, 1tr in next tr, 3ch, miss 4 tr; rep from * to last rep, ending at **, miss 2 tr, 1tr in each of next 3 tr, 1tr in top of 3-ch from previous row.

Row 18: 5ch, 11tr in next 5-ch sp, *3ch, miss 1 tr, 1tr in each of next 2 tr, miss 1 tr, 3ch, 11tr in next 5-ch sp; rep from * to last tr, 2ch, miss 1 tr, 1tr in top of 3-ch from previous row.

Row 19: 5ch, 1tr in base of 5-ch, *3ch, miss 4 tr, 1tr in next tr, 2tr in next tr, 1tr in next tr, miss 4 tr, 3ch, 1tr in next tr, 5tr, 1tr in next tr; rep from * to last 11 tr from previous row, miss 4 tr, 3ch, 1tr in next tr, 2tr in next tr, 1tr in next tr, miss 4 tr, 3ch, 1tr in third of 5-ch from previous row.
Do not fasten off.

OUTER PETALS 1, 9 AND 10:

Row 1 (RS facing): 7ch, 1dc in first tr, *3ch, miss 1 st, 1dc in next st; rep from * 7 times more, 4ch, miss 1 st, 1tr in next st.

Row 2: 7ch, 1dc in next 3-ch sp, *3ch, 1dc in next ch sp; rep from * 6 times more, 4ch, 1tr in third ch of 7-ch from previous row.

INNER PETALS 2–7:

Row 1: 5ch, 1tr in base of 5-ch, 4ch, miss 2 sts, 1dc in next st, *3ch, miss 1 st, 1dc in next st; rep from * 7 times more, 4ch, miss 2 sts, 1tr in each of next 2 sts, 5ch.

Row 2: 1tr in base of 5-ch from previous row, 4ch, 1dc in next 3-ch sp, *3ch, 1dc in next 3-ch sp; rep from * 6 times more. 4ch, 1tr in next tr, 1tr in third of 5-ch from previous row, 5ch.

Row 3: 1tr in base of 5-ch from previous row, 4ch, 1dc in next 3-ch sp, *3ch, 1dc in next 3-ch sp; rep from * 5 times more, 4ch, 1tr in next st, 1tr in third of 5-ch from previous row, 5ch.

Cont as above having one 3-ch sp less on each row until one 3-ch sp remains, ending each row with 5ch.

Next row: 1tr in base of 5-ch, 4ch, 1dc in next 3-ch sp, 4ch, 1tr in next tr, 1tr in third of 5-ch from previous row.

Next row: 5ch, 1tr in base of first 5-ch, 3ch, 1tr in next dc, 3ch, 1tr in next tr, 1tr in third of 5-ch.

Next row: 5ch, 1tr in base of first 5-ch, 3ch, 1dtr in centre tr, 3ch, 1ss in third of 5-ch.
Fasten off.

With RS facing, join in same st as last ss from previous petal and rep Petal 2.

PETAL 8:

With RS facing, join yarn in next st from ss from previous petal. Rep Petal 1.

COLLAR

Using A, make 82:**90**:98ch.

Row 1: 1dc in second ch from hook, 1dc in each ch to end. *(81:**89**:97 sts)*

Row 2: 3ch (counts as first tr), 1tr in base of first 3-ch, *2ch, miss next 2 sts, 1tr in each of next 2 sts; rep from * to end, 1ch. Do not turn.

Row 3: Yrh, insert hook in sp between 2-tr group from previous row, from behind and from back of work to front, 5tr in same sp (if you turn work to the side, it's easier to make the stitch), 1ch. Turn.

Yrh, insert hook from left to right (when row of dc is at bottom) and round back of second tr post, 5tr around second tr stem. *(1 scale made)*

*Miss next 2-tr group, insert hook around first post of next tr group (back to front), work 5tr, 1ch, insert hook from left to right and round the post of second tr, 5tr around post; rep from * to end of row. Turn.

Row 4: 3ch, 1tr in base of 3-ch, *2ch. 2tr in the centre of scale from previous row, 2ch, 2tr in centre of 2-tr group from row 2; rep from * to end scale, 2ch, 2tr in top edge of last scale, 1ch.

Row 5: Yrh, insert hook in sp between 2-tr group from previous row, from behind and from back of work to front, 5tr in same sp (if you turn work to the side, it's easier to make the stitch), 1ch. Turn.

Yrh, insert hook from left to right (when row of dc is at bottom) and round back of second tr post, 5tr around second tr post. *(1 scale made)*

*Miss next 2-tr group, insert hook around first post of next tr group (back to front), work 5tr, 1ch, insert hook from left to right and round post of second tr, 5tr around post; rep from * to end, 1ss between last 2-tr group.

Row 6: 3ch, 1tr in base of 3-ch, *2ch, 2tr in centre of scale from previous row, 2ch, 2tr in centre of 2-tr group from 2 rows before; rep from * to end, ss in last centre of scale, 1ch. Turn.

Row 7: Rep Row 3.

SIZE 24–36 MONTHS ONLY:

Rep Rows 4–5 once more.
Fasten off.

TIE

Using A and yarn doubled, make a chain approx. 76cm (30in) long.
Fasten off.

FINISHING

Fit the collar around the neck edge and sew in place.

Thread the tie on the WS of the collar by weaving it in and out of the tr groups. Using B, make two small pompoms (see page 110) and attach one on each end of the tie.

Beaded Ivory Scarf

This is worked in a delicate stitch using a soft merino yarn. The edgings have four rows of beading – see page 108 for tips on how to thread beads onto yarn and how to bead using double crochet and treble stitches.

SKILL RATING: ● ● ●

YARN AND MATERIALS

Debbie Bliss Rialto DK (100% merino wool, approx. 105m/115yd per 50g/1¾oz ball) DK (light worsted) weight yarn
   6 balls of shade 002 Ecru (off-white)

Approx. 124 x white seed beads, size 6

3.5mm (US size E/4) crochet hook

Yarn sewing needle

FINISHED MEASUREMENTS

Approx. 16.5 x 190cm (6½ x 75in)

TENSION

4 shell rows x 4 shells over a 10cm (4in) square working pattern, using a 3.5mm (US size E/4) hook and Debbie Bliss Rialto DK.

ABBREVIATIONS

approx.	approximately
ch	chain
ch sp	chain space
dc	double crochet
rep	repeat
RS	right side
sp	space
ss	slip stitch
st(s)	stitch(es)
tr	treble
WS	wrong side
yrh	yarn round hook

SPECIAL ABBREVIATIONS

V-st (V-stitch): work [1tr, 3ch, 1tr] all in same place

2trCL (2-treble cluster): *yrh, insert hook in st or sp, yrh, pull yarn through, yrh, pull through first 2 loops on hook, rep from * once more (3 loops on hook), yrh, pull yarn through all 3 loops on hook

PB (place bead): place bead following beading techniques for WS rows (see page 108)

SCARF

Make 45ch.

Row 1: 7tr in 10th ch from hook (shell), *1ch, miss 4 ch, [1tr, 1ch] in next ch, miss 4 ch, 7tr in next ch; rep from * to last 5 ch, 1ch, 1tr in last ch.

Row 2: 4ch, 1tr in first tr, *1ch, miss next 2 tr (of Shell), 1tr in each of next 3 tr, 1ch, miss next ch sp, [1tr, 3ch, 1tr] (V-st) in top of next 1tr; rep from * to last ch sp, 1ch, [1tr, 1ch, 1tr] in last ch sp.

Row 3: 3ch, 3tr in first ch sp, *1ch, miss next ch sp, [1tr, 1ch] in second tr of next 3-tr group (centre st) **, miss next 1-ch sp, 7tr in next 3-ch sp (centre of V-st); rep from * ending last rep at **, miss next ch sp, 1ch, 4tr in last ch sp.

Row 4: 3ch, miss first tr, 1tr in next tr, 1ch, miss next 2 tr and next ch sp, [1tr, 3ch, 1tr] (V-st) in next tr, *1ch, miss next ch sp and next 2 tr, 1tr in each of next 3 tr, 1ch, miss next 2 tr and next ch sp, [1tr, 3ch, 1tr] (V-st) in next tr; rep from * to last 3 tr, miss next 2 tr, 1tr in last tr, 1tr in top of first 3-ch.

Row 5: 4ch, miss first ch sp, *7tr in next 3-ch sp (centre of V-st), 1ch, miss next ch sp, [1tr, 1ch] in second tr of next 3-tr group (centre st), miss next ch sp; rep from * to last V-st, 7tr in next 3-ch sp (centre of V-st), miss last ch sp, 1ch, 1tr in top of first 3-ch.
Rep Rows 2–5 until scarf measures approx. 181.5cm (71½in) ending on a Row 5.
Fasten off.

Thread 62 beads on yarn for first edging.

EDGING SIDE 1:

Row 1 (beading row, WS): 4ch (PB on third of this 4-ch), 1tr (PB) in first tr, miss next ch sp, miss next 3 tr, *[2trCL in next tr, 3ch (PB in second of this 3-ch), 2trCL in same tr (middle of shell)], miss next 3 tr, miss next ch sp,** [1tr (PB) in next tr, 3ch (PB in second of this 3-ch), 1tr (PB)] in same tr, miss next ch sp, miss next 3 tr; rep from * ending last rep at **, [1tr (PB), 1ch, 1tr (PB)] in last ch sp.

Row 2 (RS): 4ch, 1tr in first 1ch sp, *[2trCL, 3ch, 2trCL] in next 3-ch sp** (keeping bead in between clusters), [1tr, 3ch, 1tr] in next 3-ch sp (keeping bead in between trebles); rep from * ending last rep at **, [1tr, 1ch, 1tr] in last ch sp.

Row 3 (beading row, WS): 1ch, 1dc (PB) in first tr, 2ch, *[5tr (PB), 2ch] in next 3-ch sp (between clusters, placing a bead in each tr)**, [1dc (PB), 2ch] in next 3-ch sp (between trebles); rep from * ending last rep at **, 1dc (PB) in last ch sp.

Row 4 (beading row, RS): 1ss in first dc, 1ch, *[1dc in next tr, 3ch (PB on third of these ch), ss in first of 3-ch], ss in same dc; rep from * 4 times more**. 1ch, 1dc in next dc, 1ch; rep from * 3 times more ending last rep at **, 1ch, ss in last dc.
Fasten off.

Thread 62 beads on yarn for second edging.
EDGING SIDE 2:
Working on underside of first 45ch at other end of scarf with WS facing, join yarn in first ch sp.
Row 1 (WS): 4ch (PB on third of this 4-ch), 1tr (PB) in same sp, *[2trCL in bottom sp of 7-tr shell, 3ch (PB in second of this 3-ch), 2trCL in same sp]**, [1tr (PB) in bottom of next 1-tr, 3ch (PB in second of this 3-ch), 1tr (PB] in same tr; rep from *, ending last rep at **, 1tr (PB) in 4th of first 10-ch from Row 1 of scarf, 1ch, 1tr (PB) in same place.
Rep Rows 2–4 of edging side 1.
Fasten off.

FINISHING
Sew in ends.

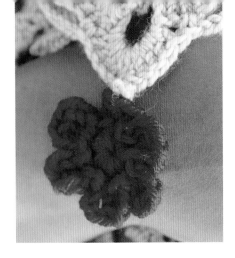

Blossom Shawl

An heirloom project with a vintage feel. This silk mix shawl is made up from individual motifs and then decorated with little flowers around the edge to give it some movement.

SKILL RATING: ● ● ●

YARN AND MATERIALS

Fyberspates Scrumptious 4ply (55% merino wool/45% silk, 365m/399yd per 100g/3½oz hank) 4ply (sport) weight yarn

  5 hanks of shade 303 Oyster (beige) (MC)
  Small amount of various shades of pink, red, and light green (CC)

3mm (US size D/3) crochet hook

Yarn sewing needle

FINISHED MEASUREMENTS

Approx. 112 x 89cm (44 x 35in)

TENSION

Tension is not critical on this project.

ABBREVIATIONS

approx.	approximately
CC	contrast colour
ch	chain
ch sp	chain space
cont	continu(e)(ing)
dc	double crochet
htr	half treble
MC	main colour
rep	repeat
sp	space
ss	slip stitch
st(s)	stitch(es)
tr	treble
WS	wrong side
yrh	yarn round hook

SPECIAL ABBREVIATIONS

3-ch picot (3-chain picot): make 3ch, ss in third ch from hook, pull tight

trCL (treble cluster): *yrh, insert hook into ring, yrh, pull yarn through, yrh, pull yarn through first 2 loops on hook; rep from * twice more (4 loops on hook), yrh, pull yarn through all 4 loops on hook

MAIN MOTIF

(make 86)
Using MC, make 8ch, join with a ss in first ch to make a ring.
Round 1: 3ch, *yrh, insert hook through ring, yrh, pull yarn through, yrh, pull yarn through 2 loops (2 loops on hook); rep from * once more (3 loops on hook), yrh, draw yarn through all 3 loops, **5ch, 1trCL into ring; rep from ** 10 times more. *(12 clusters)*
Round 2: 2ch, 1tr in top of first trCL, 1ch, *3-ch picot, 5ch, 1dc in top of next trCL; rep from * 11 times more, ss in top of first trCL from previous round.
Round 3: Take yarn behind 3-ch picot and ss in second ch of 5-ch arch, 3ch (counts as 1tr), 4tr in 5-ch sp, *5ch, [5tr in next 5-ch sp] twice; rep from * 4 times more, 5ch, 5tr in next 5-ch sp, ss into top of first 3-ch.
Round 4: Miss first st, dc in next st, 5tr in next 5-ch sp, 1ch, 3-ch picot, 5tr in same 5-ch sp, miss 2 sts, dc in next st, *7ch, miss 4 sts, 1dc in next st, 5tr in 5-ch sp, 1ch, 3-ch picot, 5tr in same 5-ch sp, miss 2 sts, 1dc in next st, rep from * 4 times more, 7ch, miss 3 sts, ss in next st.
Fasten off.

SMALL FLOWERS

(make 28 in assorted shades)
Using CC, make 4ch, join with a ss in first ch to make a ring.
6dc in ring.
*Ss in first dc, 3ch, 1tr in same st, 3ch, ss in same st; rep from * 5 times more. *(6 petals)*
Fasten off.

TIP

When you are using this yarn, always wind hanks into a ball before crocheting.

FINISHING

Lay out a row of 10 main motifs, followed by a row of 9 main motifs; repeat this sequence three more times and finish with another row of 10 motifs.

Sew the main motifs together at the points and middle chain between points.

Position and stitch a flower on each point along the long edge of the shawl and in the middle of the centre motif of the curve on the short edge.

TIP
Sew in the ends of each motif as you finish it.

Mohair Scarf

This scarf is a real show stopper – the first time I wore it three people said it was the loveliest scarf they'd seen, so it's well worth the time and effort required. It's made using a mohair silk mix, which offers some beautiful colours to choose from.

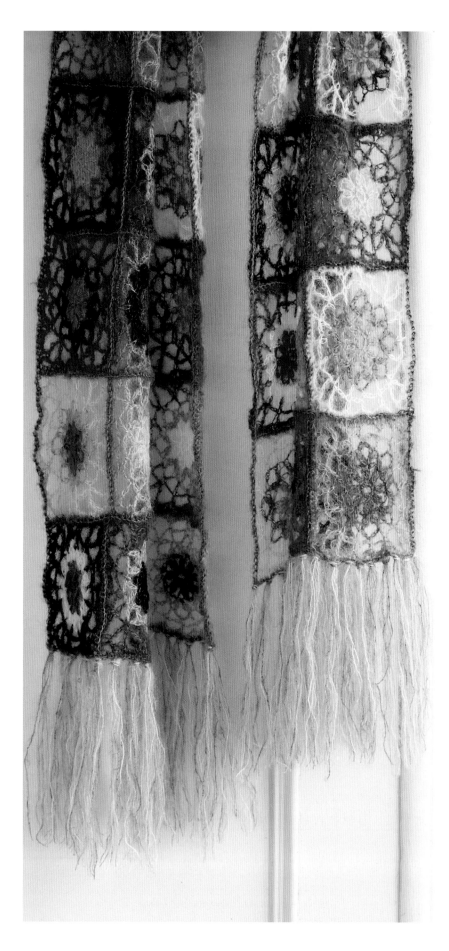

YARN AND MATERIALS

Debbie Bliss Angel (76% super kid mohair/24% silk, approx. 200m/219yd per 25g/⅞oz ball) laceweight yarn

    1 ball each of shades:
    036 Heather (light purple)
    013 Coral (deep pink)
    003 Charcoal (dark grey)
    012 Lime (pale green)
    006 Ecru (off-white)
    019 Rose (pale pink)
    009 Aqua (pale turquoise)

Rowan Kidsilk Haze (70% mohair/30% silk, approx. 210m/230yd per 25g/⅞oz ball) laceweight yarn

    1 ball each of shades:
    597 Jelly (dark green)
    641 Blackcurrant (dark purple)
    685 Laguna (teal blue)
    683 Golden Poppy (orange)

3.5mm (US size E/4) crochet hook

Yarn sewing needle

FINISHED MEASUREMENTS

Approx. 40 x 183cm (15¾ x 72in)

TENSION

Each square measures 13 x 13cm (5¼ x 5¼in), using a 3.5mm (US size E/4) crochet hook and Debbie Bliss Angel.

ABBREVIATIONS

approx.	approximately
ch	chain
ch sp(s)	chain space(s)
cont	continue
dc	double crochet
dtr	double treble
htr	half treble
rep	repeat
RS	right side
ss	slip stitch
st(s)	stitch(es)
tr	treble
yrh	yarn round hook

SPECIAL ABBREVIATIONS

2trCL (2-treble cluster): [yrh, insert hook in st, yrh, pull yarn through work, yrh, pull yarn through first 2 loops on hook] twice in same st (3 loops on hook), yrh, pull yarn through all 3 loops on hook

3trCL (3-treble cluster): [yrh, insert hook in st, yrh, pull yarn through work, yrh, pull yarn through first 2 loops on hook] 3 times in same st (4 loops on hook), yrh, pull yarn through all 4 loops on hook

Note: The scarf is made up of a total of 42 squares. Each square uses three different colours, chosen at random.

SQUARES

(make 42)

Using first colour, make 4ch, join with a ss in first ch to form a ring.

Round 1 (RS): 1ch, 8dc in ring, join with a ss in first dc. *(8 dc)*

Cont in rounds with RS always facing you.

Round 2: 3ch, 2trCL in same place as last ss (counts as 3trCL), [3ch, 3trCL in next dc] 7 times, 3ch, join with a ss in top of first 3-ch. *(8 clusters)*

Cut off first colour.

Round 3: Join second colour in loop on hook, 3ch, 1tr in same place as ss (counts as 2trCL), *miss 3 ch, [2trCL, 5ch, 2trCL] in top of next 3trCL; rep from * 6 times more, 2trCL in same place as first tr of round, 5ch, join with a ss in top of first 3-ch. *(Eight 5-ch sps)*

Cut off second colour.

Round 4: Join third colour in loop on hook, 7ch (counts as 1tr and 4ch), [1dc in next 5-ch sp, 4ch, miss next 2trCL, 1tr in next 2trCL, 4ch] 7 times, 1dc in next 5-ch sp, 4ch, join with a ss in 3rd of first 7-ch. *(Sixteen 4-ch sps)*

Round 5: Cont with third colour, 1ch, 1dc in same place as last ss, *4ch, miss 4 ch, [1dtr, 3ch, 1dtr] in next dc, 4ch, miss 4 ch, 1dc in next tr, 4ch, miss 4 ch, 1htr in next dc, 4ch, miss 4 ch, 1dc in next tr; rep from * 3 times more omitting dc at end of last rep, join with a ss in first dc.

Round 6: Cont with third colour, 1ch, 1dc in same place as last ss, 4dc in next ch sp, *[1tr, 3ch, 1tr] in next ch sp (corner), 4dc in next ch sp, 1dc in next dc, 4dc in next ch sp, 1dc in next htr, 4dc in next ch sp, 1dc in next dc, 4dc in next ch sp; rep from * twice more, [1tr, 3ch, 1tr] in next ch sp (corner), 4dc in next ch sp, 1dc in next dc, 4dc in next ch sp, 1dc in next htr, 4dc in next ch sp, join with a ss in first dc.

Fasten off.

FINISHING

Arrange the squares in three rows of 14 squares each, in a random colour order. With WS together and using light purple (36 Heather), join the squares together using a double crochet seam. First join the 14 squares in each of the three rows, then join the rows.

EDGING:

With RS facing, join light purple (36 Heather) with a ss in centre of 3-ch at one corner of scarf, 1ch, 2dc in same place, 1dc in each st and 1dc in each join along scarf edge to centre ch at next corner, *2dc in centre ch, 1dc in each st along scarf edge to centre ch at next corner; rep from * to end, join with a ss in first dc.

Fasten off.

TASSELS:

Cut 50 strands 43cm (17in) long of each of these four colours – off-white (06 Ecru), light purple (36 Heather), pale pink (19 Rose) and pale turquoise (09 Aqua).

Attach 25 tassels along each edge (see page 110). Attach the first tassel in a corner dc of edging and then a tassel in every subsequent third dc to next corner, attach last tassel in corner dc.

TIPS

Sew in the yarn ends after making each square, using a yarn sewing needle.

When adding tassels to a foundation row, make sure that you pick up at least two loops of the crochet piece and not just one loop of the foundation chain, otherwise the loop will become loose and not hold the tassel securely.

Mohair Cowl

Gorgeous, fluffy and flouncy – and this mohair cowl is also really soft and silky. Wrap it twice around your neck and it will look fantastic and keep you lovely and warm, too.

SKILL RATING: ● ● ●

YARN AND MATERIALS

Debbie Bliss Angel (76% super kid mohair/24% silk, approx. 200m/219yd per 25g/⅞oz ball) laceweight yarn
   2 balls of shade 009 Aqua (blue) (MC)
   1 ball of shade 041 Citrus (yellow) (A)

4mm (US size G/6) crochet hook

Yarn sewing needle

FINISHED MEASUREMENTS

30 x 120cm (12 x 48in), without edging

TENSION

24 sts (2 patterns) x 12 rows over a 10cm (4in) square working pattern, using a 4mm (US size G/6) hook and Debbie Bliss Angel.

ABBREVIATIONS

approx.	approximately
ch	chain
ch sp	chain space
dc	double crochet
MC	main colour
rep	repeat
RS	right side
ss	slip stitch
st(s)	stitch(es)
tch	turning chain
tr	treble

TIP

This is an easy stitch to work, but because it's in mohair it's difficult to undo if you make a mistake. Practise the stitch first on some non-hairy wool.

COWL

Using MC, make 279ch.

Row 1 (RS): 2tr in third ch from hook, *miss 2 ch, 1dc in next ch, 5ch, miss 5 ch, 1dc in next ch, miss 2 ch, 5tr in next ch; rep from * ending last rep with only 3tr in last ch.

Row 2: 1ch, 1dc in first st, *5ch, 1dc in next 5-ch sp, 5ch, 1dc in third tr of next 5-tr group; rep from * ending last rep with 1dc in top of tch.

Row 3: *5ch, 1dc in next 5-ch sp, 5tr in next dc, 1dc in next ch sp; rep from * ending 2ch, 1tr in last dc, miss tch.

Row 4: 1ch, 1dc in first st, *5ch, 1dc in third tr of next 5-tr group, 5ch, 1dc in next 5-ch sp; rep from * ending last dc in 3rd ch of last 5-ch sp.

Row 5: 3ch (counts as 1tr), 2tr in first st, *1dc in next 5-ch sp, 5ch, 1dc in next 5-ch sp, 5tr in next dc; rep from * ending last rep with only 3tr in last dc, miss tch.

Rep Rows 2, 3, 4 and 5 eight times and then Row 2 once.

Fasten off.

With RS together, join side seam using MC. Turn RS out.

BOTTOM EDGING:

With RS facing, join MC on Row 1 at seam, 5dc in each 5-ch sp, 1dc in base ch of each dc, 2dc in each 2-ch sp, 1dc in base ch of 5-tr group to end. *(276 sts)*

Join with a ss in first dc.

Fasten off.

TOP EDGING:

With RS facing, join MC at seam of final row, 5dc in each 5-ch sp, 1dc in in each dc to end. *(276 sts)*

Join with a ss in first dc.

Fasten off.

FRILL EDGE (BOTH EDGES):

With RS facing, join A, 1dc in same st, *20ch, ss in next st, 10ch, ss in next st; rep from * around, join with a ss in first dc.

Fasten off.

FINISHING

Sew in all ends.

Silk and Wool Scarf

This scarf is made using a colourful silk and soft wool mix, which is a beautiful yarn to work with and feels very smooth on the skin. The stitch is a wave and chevron stitch using trebles, with flashes of bright colour in between the blocks of colour in double crochet.

TIPS

When you are using this yarn, always wind the hanks into a ball before crocheting.

Make sure that you go into the first stitch at the beginning and end of the rows, and make the two trebles into the top of the third chain from the previous row.

At the end of each 2-row colour sequence, cut the yarn – but do not fasten off – and join in the new colour.

YARN AND MATERIALS

Fyberspates Scrumptious 4ply (55% merino wool/45% silk, 365m/399yd per 100g/3½oz hank) 4ply (sport) weight yarn

> 1 hank each of shades:
> 318 Glisten (silver) (A)
> 308 Teal Blue (dark blue) (B)
> 325 Daffodil (gold) (C)
> 310 Natural (white) (D)
> 304 Water (pale blue) (E)
> 320 Burnt Orange (bronze) (F)
> 303 Oyster (beige) (G)

3mm (US size C/2–D/3) and 4mm (US size G/6) crochet hooks

Yarn sewing needle

FINISHED MEASUREMENTS

25 x 202cm (10 x 79½in)

TENSION

24 sts x 9 rows over 10cm (4in) square working wave and chevron stitch pattern, using a 3mm (US size C/2–D/3) hook and Fyberspates Scrumptious 4ply.

ABBREVIATIONS

approx.	approximately
ch	chain
dc	double crochet
foll	following
rep	repeat
RS	right side
st(s)	stitch(es)
tr	treble
yrh	yarn round hook

SPECIAL ABBREVIATIONS

tr3tog (treble crochet 3 stitches together): *yrh, insert hook in next st, yrh, pull yarn through, yrh, pull yarn through first 2 loops on hook; rep from * in each of next 2 sts (4 loops on hook), yrh, pull yarn through all 4 loops on hook

dc3tog (double crochet 3 stitches together): [insert hook in next st, yrh, pull yarn through] 3 times, yrh, pull through all 4 loops on hook

TrRow: wave and chevron treble stitch row

DcRow: wave and chevron double crochet stitch row

SCARF

Using A and 4mm (US size G/6) hook, make 63ch.

TrRow 1: Change to 3mm (US size C/2–D/3) hook, 1tr in third ch from hook (first 2-ch counts as 1tr), 1tr in each of next 3 ch, tr3tog over next 3 ch, 1tr in each of next 3 ch, *3tr in next ch, 1tr in each of next 3 ch, tr3tog over next 3 ch, 1tr in each of next 3 ch; rep from * to last ch, 2tr in last ch.

TrRow 2: 3ch (counts as 1tr), 1tr in each of first 4 sts, tr3tog over next 3 sts, 1tr in each of next 3 sts, *3tr in next st, 1tr in each of next 3 sts, tr3tog over next 3 sts, 1tr in each of next 3 sts; rep from * to end, 2tr in top of 3-ch at end of row.

Rep TrRow 2 until 28 rows have been worked or work measures approx. 30cm (12in).

Cut yarn, do not fasten off.

DcRow1: Using 4mm (US size G/6) hook, join B, 1ch (counts as first dc), 1dc in each of first 4 sts, dc3tog over next 3 sts, 1dc in each of next 3 sts, *3dc in next st, 1dc in each of next 3 sts, dc3tog over next 3 sts, 1dc in each of next 3 sts; rep from * to end, 2dc in top of 3-ch at end of row.

DcRow2: Join C, 1ch (counts as first dc), 1dc in each of first 4 sts, dc3tog over next 3 sts, 1dc in each of next 3 sts, *3dc in next st, 1dc in each of next 3 sts, dc3tog over next 3 sts, 1dc in each of next 3 sts; rep from * to end, 2dc in top of 1-ch at end of row.

DcRow3: Join D, rep DcRow2 once more.

Cut yarn, do not fasten off.

*Using 3mm (US size C/2–D/3) hook, join E.

Rep TrRow2 until 28 rows have been worked or work measures approx. 30cm (12in), and ending first row with 2tr in top of 1-ch, and foll rows with 2tr in top of 3-ch at end of row.**

Using 4mm (US size G/6) hook, rep DcRows 1–3 using B, C and D in any order.*

Rep from * to * 4 times more, ending last rep at **, foll colour sequence F, G, E, A for TrRows.

Fasten off.

FINISHING

Sew in any ends and press lightly using a damp cloth.

Fuchsia Shawl

Mohair isn't what it used to be, it's much softer! This stunning shawl uses a lovely soft mix of mohair silk fibres. The squares are made up of lots of chain spaces and are easy to make, but it's important to practise the square first using a non-mohair yarn, because if you make a mistake with mohair it's very difficult to undo.

SKILL RATING: ● ● ●

YARN AND MATERIALS

Debbie Bliss Angel (76% super kid mohair/24% silk, approx. 200m/219yd per 25g/⅞oz ball) laceweight yarn
   3 balls of shade 045 Hot Pink (bright pink)

4mm (US size G/6) crochet hook

Yarn sewing needle

FINISHED MEASUREMENTS

22.5 x 227.5cm (9 x 91in), with tassels

TENSION

Each square measures approx. 10cm (4in), using a 4mm (US size G/6) hook and Debbie Bliss Angel.

ABBREVIATIONS

approx.	approximately
ch	chain
ch sp(s)	chain space(s)
dc	double crochet
rep	repeat
RS	right side
sp	space
ss	slip stitch
st(s)	stitch(es)
tr	treble
yrh	yarn round hook

SPECIAL ABBREVIATION

2trCL (2 treble cluster): *yrh, insert hook in st or sp, yrh, pull yarn through, yrh, pull through first 2 loops on hook, rep from * once more, yrh, pull yarn through all 3 loops on hook

SQUARES

(make 60)
Work on RS of work throughout.
Make 5ch, join with a ss to form a ring.
Round 1 (RS): 5ch (counts as 1tr, 2ch), [1tr, 2ch in ring] 7 times, join with a ss in third of first 5-ch. *(8 ch sps)*
Round 2: Ss in first ch sp, 1ch, 1dc in first ch sp, [5ch, 1dc in next ch sp] 7 times, 5ch, ss in first dc. *(8 ch sps)*
Round 3: Ss in first ch sp, 3ch, 1tr in same ch sp (counts as 2trCL), 5ch, 2trCL in same ch sp, [3ch, 1dc] in next ch sp, *[3ch, 2trCL, 5ch, 2trCL] in next ch sp, [3ch, 1dc] in next ch sp; rep from * twice more, 3ch, join with a ss in top of first tr.
Round 4: Ss in first ch sp, 3ch, 1tr in same ch sp (counts as 2trCL), 5ch, 2trCL in same ch sp, *3ch, 1dc in next ch sp, 5ch, 1dc in next ch sp, 3ch, [2trCL, 5ch, 2trCL] in next ch sp; rep from * twice more, 3ch, 1dc in next ch sp, 5ch, 1dc in next ch sp, 3ch, join with a ss in top of first tr.
Fasten off.

FINISHING

Sew in ends.

JOIN SQUARES IN SETS OF THREE:
Place two squares with RS tog, insert hook in corner 5-ch sp of both squares, *join yarn, 1ch, 1dc in same ch sp, [3ch, 1dc in next ch sp] 4 times.
Fasten off.
Open out squares. Place third square on second square with RS tog; rep from * once more.
Fasten off.
Rep until all squares are joined, making 20 sets of three.

JOIN ROWS TOGETHER:
Place two rows with RS tog, insert hook in corner 5-ch sp of both rows, join yarn, 1ch, 1dc in same ch sp, [3ch, 1dc in next ch sp] 4 times.
*At join make 2ch, 1dc in next ch sp (first ch sp of next square), [3ch, 1dc in next ch sp] 4 times; rep from * once more.
Fasten off.
Rep until all rows are joined, making 20 rows.

TASSELS:
Cut about 240 strands, each approx. 43cm (17in) long, and make each tassel with eight strands. Attach a tassel in each ch sp on the width edges (see page 110), so there are 15 tassels at each end.

TIP
Sew in ends after making each square.

Summer Evening Shawl

This is a delightful light shawl, made with a simple diamond chain stitch, and is a great project to try when you have mastered a few skills.

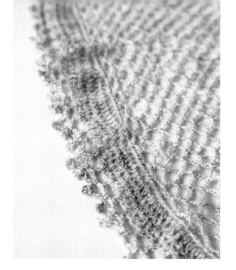

SKILL RATING: ● ● ●

YARN AND MATERIALS

Malabrigo Silkpaca (70% baby alpaca/ 30% silk, approx. 384m/420yd per 50g/1¾oz ball) laceweight yarn
  3 balls of shade SA036 Pearl (beige)

3.5mm (US size E/4) crochet hook

Yarn sewing needle

FINISHED MEASUREMENTS

Approx. 170 x 70cm (67 x 27½in)

TENSION

Tension is not critical on this project.

ABBREVIATIONS

approx.	approximately
beg	beginning
ch	chain
ch sp	chain space
cont	continue
dc	double crochet
dtr	double treble
rep	repeat
ss	slip stitch
st(s)	stitch(es)

SHAWL

Make 202ch.

Row 1: 1dc in second ch from hook, *7ch, miss 3 ch, ss in next ch; rep from * to end, make 9ch.

Row 2: *ss in third ch in centre of first 7-ch arch, 7ch; rep from * across row ending with ss in third ch of last arch, 2ch, 1dtr in last st, 8ch.

Row 3: Ss in third ch of first 7-ch arch, *7ch, ss in third ch of next arch; rep from * across, 9ch.

Rep Rows 2 and 3 until work measures approx. 162cm (64in).

Fasten off.

PICOT EDGING:

Work in rounds, not in rows. Do not turn at end of round. Place st marker at beg of each round.

Round 1: Join yarn in any st and place st marker. Work complete round of dc, working 4dc into each side and finished edge loops and 1dc in each ch of cast-on edge. Work 3dc in each corner st to make corners square. To join round, ss in first dc.

Round 2: Work another round of dc, working 1dc in each st of previous round and 3dc in each corner st. Make 2ch, ss in first dc from previous round.

Round 3: Rep Round 2.

Round 4: 6ch, miss next 2 sts, 1dc in next st, *3ch, miss next 2 sts, 1dc in next st; rep from * to end (cont to work 3dc in each corner st as previous rounds).

Round 5: 1ch, ss in first 3-ch sp, *6ch, ss in fourth ch from hook, 2ch, ss in next 3-ch sp; rep from * to end. Fasten off.

FINISHING

Sew in all ends.

Techniques

In this section, we explain how to master the simple crochet and finishing techniques that you need to make the projects in this book.

Holding the hook

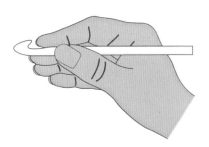

Pick up your hook as though you are picking up a pen or pencil. Keeping the hook held loosely between your fingers and thumb, turn your hand so that the palm is facing up and the hook is balanced in your hand and resting in the space between your index finger and your thumb.

You can also hold the hook like a knife – this may be easier if you are working with a large hook or with chunky yarn. Choose the method that you find most comfortable.

Holding the yarn

1 Pick up the yarn with your little finger in the opposite hand to your hook, with your palm facing upward and with the short end in front. Turn your hand to face downward, with the yarn on top of your index finger and under the other two fingers and wrapped right around the little finger, as shown above.

2 Turn your hand to face you, ready to hold the work in your middle finger and thumb. Keeping your index finger only at a slight curve, hold the work or the slip knot using the same hand, between your middle finger and your thumb and just below the crochet hook and loop/s on the hook.

Making a slip knot

The simplest way is to make a circle with the yarn, so that the loop is facing downward.

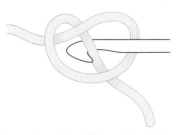

1 In one hand hold the circle at the top where the yarn crosses, and let the tail drop down at the back so that it falls across the centre of the loop. With your free hand or the tip of a crochet hook, pull a loop through the circle.

2 Put the hook into the loop and pull gently so that it forms a loose loop on the hook.

Yarn round hook (yrh)

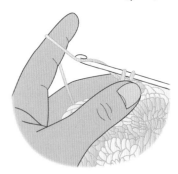

To create a stitch, catch the yarn from behind with the hook pointing upward. As you gently pull the yarn through the loop on the hook, turn the hook so it faces downward and slide the yarn through the loop. The loop on the hook should always be kept loose enough for the hook to slide through easily.

Magic ring

This is a useful starting technique if you do not want a visible hole in the centre of your round. Loop the yarn around your finger, insert the hook through the ring, yarn round hook, pull through the ring to make the first chain. Work the number of stitches required into the ring and then pull the end to tighten the centre ring and close the hole.

Slip stitch (ss)

A slip stitch doesn't create any height and it is often used as the last stitch to create a smooth and even round or row.

1 To make a slip stitch: first put the hook through the work, yarn round hook.

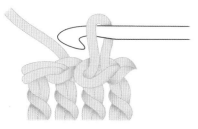

2 Pull the yarn through both the work and through the loop on the hook at the same time, so you will have 1 loop on the hook.

Chain (ch)

1 Using the hook, wrap the yarn round the hook ready to pull it through the loop on the hook.

Chain ring

If you are crocheting a round shape, one way of starting off is by crocheting a number of chains following the instructions in your pattern, and then joining them into a circle.

1 To join the chain into a circle, insert the crochet hook into the first chain that you made (not into the slip knot), yarn round hook.

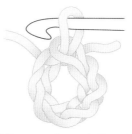

2 Pull the yarn through the chain and through the loop on your hook at the same time, thereby creating a slip stitch and forming a circle. You will now have a chain ring ready to work stitches into as instructed in the pattern.

2 Pull through, creating a new loop on the hook. Continue in this way to create a chain of the required length.

Chain space (ch sp)

1 A chain space is the space that has been made under a chain in the previous round or row, and falls in between other stitches.

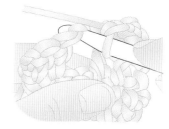

2 Stitches into a chain space are made directly into the hole created under the chain and not into the chain stitches themselves.

Making rows

When making straight rows you turn the work at the end of each row and make a turning chain to create the height you need for the stitch you are working with, as for making rounds.

Double crochet = 1 chain
Half treble crochet = 2 chains
Treble crochet = 3 chains
Double treble = 4 chains

Making rounds

When working in rounds the work is not turned, so you are always working from one side. Depending on the pattern you are working, a 'round' can be square. Start each round by making one or more chains to create a turning chain to the height you need for the stitch you are working:

Double crochet = 1 chain
Half treble crochet = 2 chains
Treble crochet = 3 chains
Double treble = 4 chains
Work the required stitches to complete the round. At the end of the round, slip stitch into the top of the chain to close the round.

If you work in a spiral you do not need a turning chain. After completing the base ring, place a stitch marker in the first stitch and then continue to crochet around. When you have made a round and reached the point where the stitch marker is, work this stitch, take out the stitch marker from the previous round and put it back into the first stitch of the new round. A safety pin or piece of yarn in a contrasting colour makes a good stitch marker.

How to measure a tension (gauge) square

Using the hook and the yarn recommended in the pattern, make a number of chains to measure approximately 15cm (6in). Working in the stitch pattern given for the tension measurements, work enough rows to form a square. Fasten off.

Take a ruler, place it horizontally across the square and, using pins, mark a 10cm (4in) area. Repeat vertically to form a 10cm (4in) square on the fabric.

Count the number of stitches across, and the number of rows within the square, and compare against the tension given in the pattern.

If your numbers match the pattern, then use this size hook and yarn for your project. If you have more stitches, then your tension is tighter than recommended and you need to use a larger hook. If you have fewer stitches, then your tension is looser and you will need a smaller hook.

Make tension squares using different size hooks until you have matched the tension in the pattern, and use this hook to make the project.

Double crochet (dc)

1 Insert the hook into your work, yarn round hook and pull the yarn through the work only (2 loops on the hook).

2 Yarn round hook again and pull through the 2 loops on the hook. (1 loop on the hook). One double crochet made.

Half treble crochet (htr)

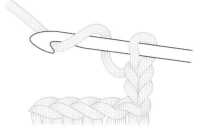  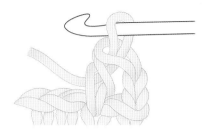

1 Before inserting the hook into the work, wrap the yarn round the hook and put the hook through the work with the yarn wrapped around.

2 Yarn round hook again and pull through the first loop on the hook (3 loops on the hook).

3 Yarn round hook and pull the yarn through all 3 loops (1 loop on the hook). One half treble crochet made.

Treble crochet (tr)

1 Before inserting the hook into the work, wrap the yarn round the hook. Put the hook through the work with the yarn wrapped around, yarn round hook again and pull through the first loop on the hook (3 loops on the hook).

2 Yarn round hook again, pull the yarn through the first 2 loops on the hook (2 loops on the hook).

3 Pull the yarn through 2 loops again (1 loop on the hook). One treble crochet made.

Double treble (dtr)

Yarn round hook twice, insert the hook into the stitch, yarn round hook, pull a loop through (4 loops on hook), yarn round hook, pull the yarn through 2 stitches (3 loops on hook), yarn round hook, pull a loop through the next 2 stitches (2 loops on hook), yarn round hook, pull a loop through the last 2 stitches (1 loop on the hook). One double treble made.

Triple treble (ttr)

Triple trebles are 'tall' stitches and are an extension on the basic treble stitch. They need a turning chain of 5 chains.

1 Yarn round hook 3 times, insert the hook into the stitch or space. Yarn round hook, pull the yarn through the work (5 loops on the hook).

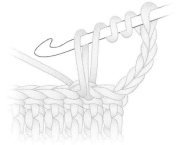

2 Yarn round hook, pull the yarn through the first 2 loops on the hook (4 loops on the hook).

3 Yarn round hook, pull the yarn through the first 2 loops on the hook (3 loops on the hook).

4 Yarn round hook, pull the yarn through the first 2 loops on the hook (2 loops on hook). Yarn round hook, pull the yarn through the 2 loops on the hook (1 loop on the hook). One triple treble made.

Quadruple treble (qtr)

For qtr, begin by wrapping the yarn round the hook 4 times and then proceed in the same way as for triple treble (above) until you are left with 1 loop on the hook. One quadruple treble made.

Increasing

Make two or three stitches into one stitch or space from the previous row. The illustration shows a treble crochet increase being made.

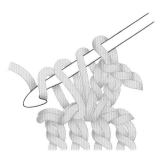

Decreasing

You can decrease by either missing the next stitch and continuing to crochet, or by crocheting two or more stitches together. The basic technique for crocheting stitches together is the same, no matter which stitch you are using.

DOUBLE CROCHET TWO STITCHES TOGETHER (DC2TOG)

1 Insert the hook into your work, yarn round hook and pull the yarn through the work (2 loops on hook). Insert the hook in next stitch, yarn round hook and pull the yarn through.

2 Yarn round hook again and pull through all 3 loops on the hook. You will then have 1 loop on the hook.

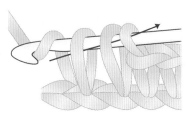

DOUBLE CROCHET THREE STITCHES TOGETHER (DC3TOG)

1 Insert the hook in the stitch, yarn round hook, pull the yarn through the work (2 loops on hook).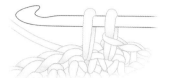

2 Insert the hook in the next stitch, yarn round hook, pull the yarn through the work (3 loops on hook).

3 Insert the hook in the next stitch, yarn round hook, pull the yarn through the work (4 loops on hook).

4 Yarn round hook, pull the yarn through all 4 loops on the hook (1 loop on hook). One double crochet three stitches together made.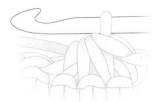

HALF TREBLE 2 STITCHES TOGETHER (HTR2TOG)

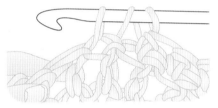 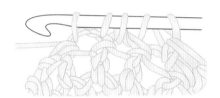 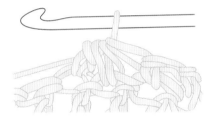

1 Yarn round hook, insert the hook into the next stitch, yarn round hook, draw the yarn through (3 loops on the hook).

2 Yarn round hook, insert the hook into the next stitch, yarn round hook, draw the yarn through the work (5 loops on the hook).

3 Yarn round hook, draw the yarn through all 5 loops on the hook (1 loop on hook).

TREBLE CROCHET 3 STITCHES TOGETHER (TR3TOG)

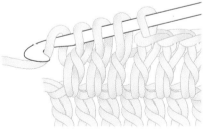

Work a treble into each of the next three stitches as normal, but leave the last loop of each stitch on the hook (4 loops on the hook). Yarn round hook and pull the yarn through all the stitches on the hook to join them together (1 loop on the hook).

Clusters

Clusters are groups of stitches, with each stitch only partly worked and then all joined at the end to form one stitch that creates a particular pattern and shape. They are most effective when made using a longer stitch such as a treble. Clusters can be made with any number of stitches and there can be variations in the exact way they are worked, so follow the special abbreviation instructions in each pattern.

CLUSTER (CL)

1 Yarn round hook, insert the hook in the stitch. Yarn round hook, pull the yarn through the work. Yarn round hook, insert the hook in the same stitch.

2 Yarn round hook, pull the yarn through the work. Yarn round hook, insert the hook in the same stitch. Yarn round hook, pull the yarn through the work. Yarn round hook (7 loops on the hook). Pull the yarn through all 7 loops on the hook. Yarn round hook, one cluster made.

TWO-TREBLE CLUSTER (2TRCL)

1 Yarn round hook, insert the hook in the stitch (or space). Yarn round hook, pull the yarn through the work (3 loops on the hook).

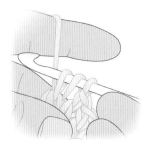

2 Yarn round hook, pull the yarn through 2 loops on the hook (2 loops on the hook). Yarn round hook, insert the hook in the same stitch (or space).

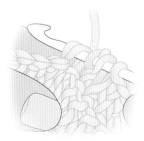

3 Yarn round hook, pull the yarn through the work (4 loops on the hook). Yarn round hook, pull the yarn through 2 loops on the hook (3 loops on the hook).

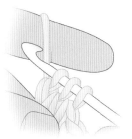

4 Yarn round hook, pull the yarn through all 3 loops on the hook (1 loop on the hook). One two-treble cluster made.

THREE-TREBLE CLUSTER (3TRCL)

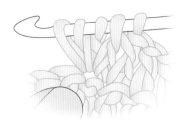

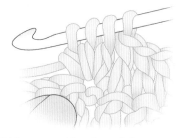

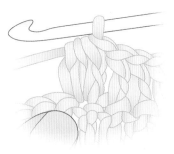

1 Work as 2trCL to end of step 3. Yarn round hook, insert the hook in the same stitch (or space), yarn round hook, pull the yarn through the work (5 loops on the hook).

2 Yarn round hook, pull the yarn through 2 loops on the hook (4 loops on the hook).

3 Yarn round hook, pull the yarn through all 4 loops on the hook (1 loop on the hook). One three-treble cluster made.

Special stitches

RAISED TREBLE ROUND FRONT (TR/RF)

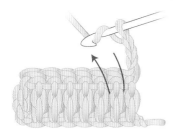 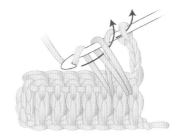 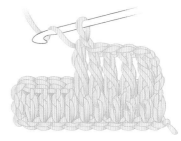

1 Yarn round hook and insert the hook from the front and around the post (the stem) of the next treble from right to left.

2 Yarn round hook and pull the yarn through the work, yarn round hook and pull the yarn through the first 2 loops on the hook.

3 Yarn round hook and pull the yarn through the 2 loops on the hook (1 loop on the hook). One raised treble round front completed.

RAISED TREBLE ROUND BACK (TR/RB)

 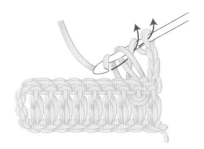 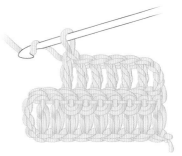

1 Yarn round hook and insert the hook from the back and around the post (the stem) of the next treble as directed in the pattern from right to left.

2 Yarn round hook and pull the yarn through the work, yarn round hook and pull the yarn through the first 2 loops on the hook.

3 Yarn round hook and pull the yarn through the 2 loops on the hook (1 loop on the hook). One raised treble round back completed.

FANS

Fans are groups of stitches worked into the same stitch to create a V-shape fan-like effect. In the Lace Scarf on page 68 the fan group worked is 3 trebles, 1 chain, 3 trebles (3tr, 1ch, 3tr) all worked into the same place.

V STITCH (V-ST)

V stitches are also groups of stitches that resemble a V shape but they have fewer stitches than fans. V stitches can have different combinations of stitches, but they are usually one stitch followed by a chain and a repeat of the first stitch on the other side of the chain. In the Lace Scarf on page 68 the V stitch is 1 half treble, 1 chain, 1 half treble (1htr, 1ch, 1htr) all worked into the same place.

Beading

THREADING BEADS ONTO YARN

All the beads must be threaded onto the yarn before you start crocheting. If you run out of beads and need to add more, you will need to cut the yarn at the end of the row/round and thread more beads onto the ball and then join in the yarn again to continue. If the beads need to be placed in order, begin threading with the last one to be used first, so it will come up to the hook last. The size of the bead hole is usually too small for a yarn sewing needle eye to go through, and the yarn is too thick to be threaded onto a normal sewing needle, so here is a technique to thread the beads onto the yarn.

1 Make a loop with some cotton sewing thread and thread a sewing needle with the loop (not the end). Leave the loop hanging approx. 2.5cm (1in) from the eye of the needle. Pull the yarn end through the loop of the thread.

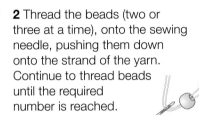

2 Thread the beads (two or three at a time), onto the sewing needle, pushing them down onto the strand of the yarn. Continue to thread beads until the required number is reached.

Beads are placed when working with the wrong side of the work facing you. The beads will sit at the back of the work, and so appear on the front (right side).

PLACING A BEAD WITH DOUBLE CROCHET

1 Work with the wrong side of the work facing you. Insert the hook into the stitch, yarn round hook, pull the yarn through the stitch (2 loops on the hook), slide the bead up the yarn strand so it is close to the back of the work.

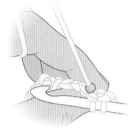

2 Yarn round hook, pull the yarn through both loops on the hook. The bead is now placed at the back of the work, so will be on the front or the right side of the final piece.

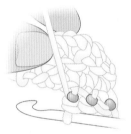

PLACING A BEAD WITH TREBLE CROCHET

1 Work with the wrong side of the work facing you. Yarn round hook, insert the hook into the stitch, yarn round hook, pull the yarn through the stitch (3 loops on the hook), yarn round hook, pull the yarn through the first two loops on the hook (2 loops on the hook). Slide the bead up the yarn strand and place it close to the back of the work.

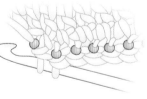

2 Yarn round hook, pull the yarn through both loops on the hook. The bead is now placed at the back of the work, so will be on the front or the right side of the final piece.

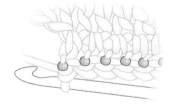

Joining yarn at the end of a row or round

You can use this technique when changing colour, or when joining in a new ball of yarn as one runs out.

1 Keep the loop of the old yarn on the hook. Drop the tail and catch a loop of the strand of the new yarn with the crochet hook.

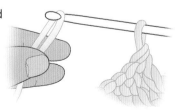

2 Draw the new yarn through the loop on the hook, keeping the old loop drawn tight and continue as instructed in the pattern.

Fastening off

Fastening off is important to stop the work from unravelling. You must cut the yarn first and then thread the tail through the loop. Pull the loop firmly and leave an end long enough to sew in the end afterwards. An end of 10–15cm (4–6in) is generally long enough, but make this the minimum length of tail – it may be best to leave ends slightly longer if using thick or chunky yarns.

TO 'CUT OFF YARN'

You will be instructed to cut off (or break) the yarn if the work hasn't finished and a new colour needs to be joined. When this instruction is given in your crochet pattern, do not fasten off the loop on your crochet hook. Simply cut the yarn at least 10cm (4in) from the work and leave the loop on the hook. Then continue following the instructions for what to do next.

TO 'FASTEN OFF' A PIECE OF CROCHET

Cut the yarn, leaving a yarn tail of at least 10cm (4in). Using the hook, pull the yarn tail all the way through the loop and pull tightly.

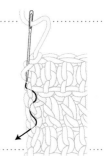

Weaving in yarn ends

It is important to weave in the tail ends of the yarn so that they are secure and your crochet won't unravel. Thread a yarn needle with the tail end of yarn. On the wrong side, take the needle through the crochet one stitch down on the edge, then take it through the stitches, working in a gentle zig-zag. Work through four or five stitches then return in the opposite direction. Remove the needle, pull the crochet gently to stretch it and trim the end.

Making an oversewn seam

An oversewn join gives a nice flat seam and is the simplest and most common joining technique.

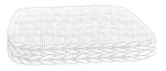

1 Thread a yarn needle with the yarn you're using in the project. Place the pieces to be joined with right sides together.

2 Insert the needle in one corner in the top loops of the stitches of both pieces and pull up the yarn, leaving a tail of about 5cm (2in). Go into the same place with the needle and pull up the yarn again; repeat two or three times to secure the yarn at the start of the seam.

3 Join the pieces together by taking the needle through the loops at the top of corresponding stitches on each piece to the end. Fasten off the yarn at the end, as in step 2.

Making a double crochet seam

With a double crochet seam you join two pieces together using a crochet hook and working a double crochet stitch through both pieces, instead of sewing them together with a tail of yarn and a yarn sewing needle. This makes a quick and strong seam and gives a slightly raised finish to the edging. For a less raised seam, follow the same basic technique, but work each stitch in slip stitch rather than double crochet.

1 Start by lining up the two pieces with wrong sides together. Insert the hook in the top 2 loops of the stitch of the first piece, then into the corresponding stitch on the second piece.

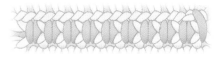

2 Complete the double crochet stitch as normal and continue on the next stitches as directed in the pattern. This gives a raised effect if the double crochet stitches are made on the right side of the work.

3 You can work with the wrong side of the work facing (with the pieces right side facing) if you don't want this effect and it still creates a good strong join.

Pompoms

CARDBOARD RING METHOD

This method can be used to make medium to large pompoms.

1 Using a pair of card rings cut to the size pompom you would like to create, cut a length of yarn and wind it around the rings until the hole in the centre is filled.

2 Cut through the loops around the outer edge of the rings and ease slightly apart. Thread a length of yarn between the layers and tie tightly, leaving a long end. Remove the card rings and fluff up the pompom. The long yarn tail can be used to sew the pompom in place.

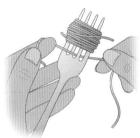

FORK METHOD

For small pompoms, use this fun method.

1 Keeping the yarn attached to the ball, wrap it around a fork about twenty times. Keep the wraps tight, and centre them in the middle of the fork, leaving space at the top and bottom.

2 Cut the yarn and hold the wraps in place on the fork. Cut a 7.5cm (3in) length of yarn and thread it through the middle of the fork at the bottom from front to back.

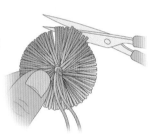

3 Wrap one end around and back over the top until the ends meet, then tie them tightly together at the front. Wrap the tie around the centre a few more times and tie another knot at the back.

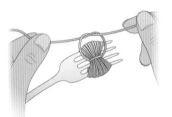

4 Pull the wrap off the fork and pull the knot tighter. The wrap will begin to curl and turn flat and round. Tie a knot on top of the first to secure. Use sharp embroidery scissors to cut the loops on either side of the tie. Trim and fluff it up to a round, even shape.

Tassels

Tassels are single clusters of knotted yarn ends; if they are repeated close together along an edge this creates a fringe. Use the same colour yarn as for your project, or choose a contrast colour of your choice.

1 Cut strands of yarn to the length given in the pattern. Take one or more strands and fold in half. With the right side of the project facing, insert a crochet hook in one of the edge stitches from the wrong side. Catch the bunch of strands with the hook at the fold point.

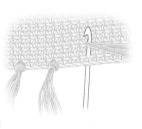

2 Draw all the loops through the stitch.

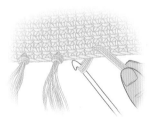

3 Pull through to make a big loop and, using your fingers, pull the tails of the bunch of strands through the loop.

4 Pull on the tails to tighten the loop firmly to secure the tassel.

Embroidery stitches

STRAIGHT STITCH

These are single straight stitches that are not placed in a straight line but used at an appropriate angle to create whiskers for the Nugget the Mouse hat on page 12.

SATIN STITCH

To work satin stitch, it can help to outline the shape you want to fill first. Then begin at one end of the shape and work straight stitches from side to side, placed very close together and varying their length as required to create a solid shape.

FRENCH KNOTS

1 Thread the yarn into a yarn needle. Bring the yarn out at your starting point from the back of the work to the front and where you want the French knot to sit, leaving a tail of yarn at the back that you will sew in later. Pick up a couple of strands across the stitch on the front of the work close to the place the yarn has been pulled through.

2 Wrap the yarn round the needle two or three times, pushing the wraps close to the crochet piece. The more wraps you make, the bigger the knot will be.

3 Take the needle in one hand and pull it through the wraps, holding the wraps in place near the crochet piece with the other hand. This forms a little knot close to the crochet piece.

4 Insert the needle (from the right side) very close to the knot and push the needle through to the wrong side to finish.

Crochet Stitch Conversion Chart

Crochet stitches are worked in the same way in both the UK and the USA, but the stitch names are not the same and identical names are used for different stitches. See right for a list of the UK terms used in this book, and the equivalent US terms.

UK TERM	US TERM
double crochet (dc)	single crochet (sc)
half treble (htr)	half double crochet (hdc)
treble (tr)	double crochet (dc)
double treble (dtr)	treble (tr)
triple treble (ttr)	double treble (dtr)
quadruple treble (qtr)	triple treble (ttr)
tension	gauge
yarn round hook (yrh)	yarn over hook (yoh)

Abbreviations

alt	alternat(e)ing	**g**	gram(mes)	**st(s)**	stitch(es)
approx.	approximately	**htr**	half treble	**tog**	together
beg	beginning	**in**	inch(es)	**tr**	treble
CC	contrast colour	**inc**	increas(e)ing	**tr/rb**	raised treble round back
CL	cluster	**m**	metre(s)	**tr/rf**	raised treble round front
cm	centimetre(s)	**MC**	main colour	**ttr**	triple treble
cont	continu(e)ing	**mm**	millimetre(s)	**yd**	yard(s)
ch	chain	**oz**	ounce(s)	**WS**	wrong side
ch sp	chain space	**PM**	place marker	**yrh**	yarn round hook
dc	double crochet	**prev**	previous	**[ ]**	work section between
dc2tog	double crochet 2 stitches together	**qtr**	quadruple treble		square brackets number of times stated
dec	decreas(e)ing	**rem**	remaining		
dtr	double treble	**rep**	repeat	*****	asterisk indicates beginning of repeated section of pattern
foll	follow(s)ing	**RS**	right side		
		ss	slip stitch		

Suppliers

For reasons of space we cannot cover all stockists, so please explore the local yarn shops and online stores in your own country.

UK

Love Crochet
www.lovecrafts.com

Wool
+44 (0)1225 469144
www.woolbath.co.uk

VV Rouleaux
+44 (0)207 224 5179
www.vvrouleaux.com

Deramores
www.deramores.com

Laughing Hens
www.laughinghens.com

John Lewis
www.johnlewis.com

Hobbycraft
www.hobbycraft.co.uk

USA

Knitting Fever Inc.
www.knittingfever.com

WEBS
www.yarn.com

Jo-Ann Fabric and Craft Stores
www.joann.com

Michaels
www.michaels.com

AUSTRALIA

Black Sheep Wool 'n' Wares
Tel: +61 (0)2 6779 1196
www.blacksheepwool.com.au

Sun Spun
Tel: +61 (0)3 9830 1609
www.sunspun.com.au

If you wish to substitute a different yarn for the one recommended in the pattern, try the Yarnsub website for suggestions:
www.yarnsub.com

Index

abbreviations 111
animal hats
    Neil the tiger 58–61
    Nugget the mouse 12–14

babies
    baby beanie hat with
        flowers 10–11
    baby's flower bonnet
        54–7
    baby's pompom hat 22–3
    baby's sailboat hat 62–3
    Neil the tiger 58–61
    Nugget the mouse 12–14
    ribbon baby hat 32–3
    tasselled baby poncho
        46–7
beading 108
    beaded ivory scarf 84–5
beanie hats 52–3
    baby beanie hat with
        flowers 10–11
    baby's sailboat hat 62–3
    pompom beanie hat 27–9
blossom shawl 86–8
bonnet, baby's flower 54–7

cape, red petal 80–3
chain (ch) 101
chain ring 101
chain space (ch sp) 101
chevron and daisy scarf
    66–7
clusters 106
conversion chart 111
cowl, mohair 92–3
crochet hooks, holding 100

decreasing 104–5
double crochet (dc) 102
double treble (dtr) 103

ear flap hat 15–17
embroidery stitches 111

fans 107
fastening off 109
flowers
    baby beanie hat with
        flowers 10–11
    baby's flower bonnet
        54–7
    blossom shawl 86–8
    chevron and daisy scarf
        66–7
    ear flap hat 15–17
    floral lace scarf 71–3
    peaked toddler hat 24–6
    red petal cape 80–3
    ribbon baby hat 32–3
    rose headband 18–19
French knots 111

fuchsia shawl 96–7

half treble crochet (htr) 103
hats
    baby beanie hat with
        flowers 10–11
    baby's flower bonnet
        54–7
    baby's pompom hat 22–3
    baby's sailboat hat 62–3
    beanie hat 52–3
    ear flap hat 15–17
    Neil the tiger 58–61
    Nugget the mouse 12–14
    peaked toddler hat 24–6
    pompom beanie hat 27–9
    ribbon baby hat 32–3
    ribbon hat 20–1
headbands
    rose headband 18–19
    turban headband 30–1

increasing 104

lace scarves 68–70
    floral lace scarf 71–3

magic ring 101
mohair
    mohair cowl 92–3
    mohair scarf 89–91

neckerchief, textured 38–9
Neil the tiger 58–61
Nugget the mouse 12–14

peaked toddler hat 24–6
pompoms 110
    baby's pompom hat 22–3
    pompom beanie hat 27–9
poncho, tasselled baby
    46–7

quadruple treble (qtr) 104

raised treble round back
    (TR/RB) 107
raised treble round front
    (TR/RF) 107
red petal cape 80–3
ribbons
    ribbon baby hat 32–3
    ribbon hat 20–1
rose headband 18–19
rounds, making 102
rows, making 102

sailboat hat, baby's 62–3
satin stitch 111
scarves
    beaded ivory scarf 84–5
    chevron and daisy scarf
        66–7

chunky patchwork scarf
    36–7
chunky scarf 42–3
chunky seashell scarf
    78–9
floral lace scarf 71–3
lace scarf 68–70
mohair scarf 89–91
silk and wool scarf 94–5
skinny scarf 44–5
swishy scarf 76–7
tweedy scarf 40–1
wave and chevron
    chunky scarf 48–9
wave and chevron stitch
    scarf 74–5
seams
    double crochet 109
    oversewn 109
seashell scarf, chunky 78–9
shawls
    blossom shawl 86–8
    fuchsia shawl 96–7
    summer evening shawl
        98–9
silk and wool scarf 94–5
skinny scarf 44–5
slip knots 100
slip stitch (sl st) 101
stitches
    embroidery stitches 111
    special stitches 107
straight stitch 111
summer evening shawl
    98–9
swishy scarf 76–7

tassels 110
    tasselled baby poncho
        46–7
techniques 100–11
tension (gauge) squares
    102
textured neckerchief 38–9
toddler hat, peaked 24–6
treble crochet (tr) 103
triple treble (ttr) 104
turban headband 30–1
tweedy scarf 40–1

V stitch (V-ST) 107

waves and chevrons
    wave and chevron
        chunky scarf 48–9
    wave and chevron stitch
        scarf 74–5

yarn
    holding 100
    joining 108
yarn ends, weaving in 109
yarn round hook (yrh) 100